Like a Phoenix

*Cycle B Sermons for Pentecost Through Proper 15
Based on the Gospel Lesson Texts*

Dean Feldmeyer

CSS Publishing Company, Inc.
Lima, Ohio

LIKE A PHOENIX
CYCLE B SERMONS FOR PENTECOST SUNDAY THROUGH PROPER 15
BASED ON GOSPEL LESSON TEXTS

FIRST EDITION
Copyright © 2017
by CSS Publishing Co., Inc.

Published by CSS Publishing Company, Inc., Lima, Ohio 45807. All rights reserved. No part of this publication may be reproduced in any manner whatsoever without the prior permission of the publisher, except in the case of brief quotations embodied in critical articles and reviews. Inquiries should be addressed to: CSS Publishing Company, Inc., Permissions Department, 5450 N. Dixie Highway, Lima, Ohio 45807.

Scripture quotations marked (NRSV) are from the New Revised Standard Version of the Bible. Copyright 1989 by the Division of Christian Education of the National Council of the Churches of Christ in the USA, Nashville, Thomas Nelson Publishers © 1989. Used by permission. All rights reserved.

Library of Congress Cataloging-in-Publication Data

Names: Feldmeyer, Dean, 1916- author.
Title: Like a phoenix : Cycle B sermons for Pentecost through Proper 14 : based on the gospel lesson texts / Dean Feldmeyer.
Description: FIRST EDITION. | Lima, Ohio : CSS Publishing Company, Inc., 2017.
Identifiers: LCCN 2017009722| ISBN 9780788028991 (pbk. : alk. paper) | ISBN 0788028995 (pbk. : alk. paper)
Subjects: LCSH: Bible. Mark--Sermons. | Bible. John--Sermons. | Pentecost--Sermons. | Common lectionary (1992). Year B.
Classification: LCC BS2585.54 .F45 2017 | DDC 252/.64--dc23
LC record available at https://lccn.loc.gov/2017009722

For more information about CSS Publishing Company resources, visit our website at www.csspub.com, email us at csr@csspub.com, or call (800) 241-4056.

e-book:
ISBN-13: 978-0-7880-2900-2
ISBN-10: 0-7880-2900-4

ISBN-13: 978-0-7880-2899-5
ISBN-10: 0-7880-2899-1   PRINTED IN USA

For Jean

Table of Contents

Pentecost Sunday — 7
  Together in One Place
  Acts 2:1-21

Trinity Sunday — 19
  Meeting Jesus
  John 3:1-17

Proper 5 — 29
  Meet the Rose Family
  Mark 3:20-35

Proper 6 — 37
  Little Start, Big Finish
  Mark 4:26-34

Proper 7 — 47
  A Non-anxious Presence
  Mark 4:35-41

Proper 8 — 57
  Desperation to Hope
  Mark 5:21-43

Proper 9 — 67
  Like a Phoenix
  Mark 6:1-13

Proper 10 — 77
  Promises to Keep
  Mark 6:14-29

Proper 11 87
Missional Discontinuity
Mark 6:30-34, 53-56

Proper 12 97
More than Enough
John 6:1-21

Proper 13 109
Never on Sunday
Mark 2:23—3:6

Proper 14 121
Metaphors Be with You
John 6:35, 41-51

Proper 15 131
"Living Bread"
John 6:51-58

Appendix 141

Pentecost Sunday
Acts 2:1-21

Together in One Place

When the day of Pentecost had come, they were all together in one place. And suddenly from heaven there came a sound like the rush of a violent wind, and it filled the entire house where they were sitting. Divided tongues, as of fire, appeared among them, and a tongue rested on each of them. All of them were filled with the Holy Spirit and began to speak in other languages, as the Spirit gave them ability. Now there were devout Jews from every nation under heaven living in Jerusalem. And at this sound the crowd gathered and was bewildered, because each one heard them speaking in the native language of each. Amazed and astonished, they asked, "Are not all these who are speaking Galileans? And how is it that we hear, each of us, in our own native language? Parthians, Medes, Elamites, and residents of Mesopotamia, Judea and Cappadocia, Pontus and Asia, Phrygia and Pamphylia, Egypt and the parts of Libya belonging to Cyrene, and visitors from Rome, both Jews and proselytes, Cretans and Arabs — in our own languages we hear them speaking about God's deeds of power." All were amazed and perplexed, saying to one another, "What does this mean?" But others sneered and said, "They are filled with new wine." But Peter, standing with the eleven, raised his voice and addressed them: "Men of Judea and all who live in Jerusalem, let this be known to you, and listen to what I say. Indeed, these are not drunk, as you suppose, for it is only nine o'clock in the morning. No, this is what was spoken through the prophet Joel: 'In the last days it will be, God declares, that I will pour out my Spirit upon all flesh, and your sons and your daughters shall prophesy, and your young men shall see visions, and your old men shall dream dreams. Even upon my slaves, both men and women, in those days I will pour out my Spirit; and they shall prophesy. And I will show portents in the heaven above and signs on the earth below, blood,

and fire, and smoky mist. The sun shall be turned to darkness and the moon to blood, before the coming of the Lord's great and glorious day. Then everyone who calls on the name of the Lord shall be saved.'"
— Acts 2:1-21

Church: Definition and Purpose

Today, Pentecost Sunday, is the day upon which we traditionally celebrate the birth of the Christian church. But before we light the candles and sing, "Happy Birthday," perhaps we should take a few moments to talk about what the church is and what it isn't.

What, exactly, is a church? How shall we define it and how shall we define its purpose?

The Internal Revenue Code uses the word "church" but it doesn't actually define what it means by that word. Certain attributes of a church have been developed by the IRS and by court decisions, however, for determining if an entity is or is not a church. Here is a list of some of those attributes:

- Distinct legal existence
- Recognized creed and form of worship
- Definite and distinct ecclesiastical government
- Formal code of doctrine and discipline
- Distinct religious history
- Membership that is not associated with any other church or denomination
- An organization of ordained ministers
- Ordained ministers selected after completing prescribed courses of study
- Literature of its own
- Established places of worship
- Regular congregations

- Regular religious services
- Sunday schools for the religious instruction of the young
- Schools for the preparation of its members

The IRS generally uses a combination of these characteristics, together with other facts and circumstances, to determine whether an organization is considered a church for federal tax purposes.[1]

The United Methodist church is a little more specific than the IRS. Here's how we describe and define the church and its purpose:

> ... the Church is of God,
> And will be preserved to the end of time,
> For the conduct of worship
> and the due administration of the sacraments,
> the maintenance of Christian fellowship and discipline,
> the edification of believers,
> and the conversion of the world.
> All, of every age and station,
> stand in need of the means of grace which it alone supplies.[2]

I did a little, informal survey of my colleagues and friends in our community and, it turns out, most churches have a doctrinal statement or a ritual something like this that defines their understanding of the nature and purpose of the church. Not just their church, but the church of Jesus Christ in the world.

Today, as we celebrate the birth of the church about 1985 years ago, give or take, it is appropriate that we should also stop for a few minutes to ask what the church is, what is its purpose and how it came to be. We'll start with that last question, first. How did the church come to be?

Pentecost

The Reverend Dr. Mark D. Roberts provides an excellent little tutorial on the history and meaning of Pentecost in the blog that he writes for the religion website, *Patheos.com*. I won't read you his entire article but here are some of the highlights:

The word, Pentecost, is an English transliteration of the Greek word *pentekostos*, which means, "fifty."

In the book of Leviticus (23:16), which is the book that lays out all of the early Hebrew religious rites and celebrations, the people of YHWH are told that they are to count fifty days from Passover and, on that day a celebration or feast is to be held to give thanks to God for the spring harvest. The feast day later became a weeklong festival surrounding that fiftieth day.

Since fifty days is, roughly, seven weeks, the feast day was also called the "Feast of Weeks" or just "Weeks." (In Hebrew *Shavuot* = weeks.)

As the Hebrew religion evolved through 500 years into Judaism the feast also came to be the time for celebrating the giving of the Law to the people, by YHWH, through Moses on Mount Sinai.

By the time Luke was writing the book of Acts, thousands of Jewish people from all over the eastern world came to Jerusalem to participate in the festival. And it was at this time, under these conditions, that the Spirit of God was poured out upon the followers of Jesus.

Luke describes it in *The Acts of the Apostles*, like this:

He begins by briefly setting the stage. It's the day of Pentecost and "they were all together in one place."

They were all Jews so, presumably, they had all come together to celebrate the Feast of Weeks with other Jews in Jerusalem at or near the temple. But on this day they are not at, or not yet at, the temple.

They had come together in some other place, a house — maybe for a meal, maybe just to chat, or maybe to bathe in that experience of being together with people who have the same experiences, the same outlook, the same point of view.

We have all had that experience, haven't we? We seem to know, instinctively, that while there's nothing wrong with being alone, being together is better. Perhaps you have received good news while you were alone and you just had to call someone to share it with them, not because they necessarily wanted or needed to know about it, but because your own joy is increased so much when you share it with someone else.

Or maybe you were having a bad day of disappointments and mishaps and you called someone to talk to not because they had a magic answer that would solve your problems but simply because sharing troubles and strife seems to shrink them to manageable size.

Whatever the reason, they had all come together in one place. Luke has said earlier that there were about 120 followers of Jesus by this time, just seven weeks after his crucifixion and resurrection, but it's hard to imagine that many people gathered together in one first-century Jerusalem home. Modern historians and sociologists put the number at a more realistic 35-40.

However many they were, the point is not the size of the crowd but their behavior. *They were all together in one place.* Do you realize how phenomenal that is, how rare and powerful it is? I have been a minister for 35 years and served six churches that ranged in size from 60 to 1,200 and I have never, not once, seen that happen — all of the members of the church together in one place at the same time.

And it's *so* important!

We know this instinctively as families, don't we? We know that to keep the family intact we need, from time to time, to come together in one place. Usually this happens at holidays or family reunions and Hollywood is fond of depicting these times as though they were torture to be endured. But the fact is, many of our families are made stronger and bonded more firmly together because of these times that we have spent together, eating, laughing, playing, singing, retelling the same old stories, and sometimes just being in the presence of those we love and who love us. It isn't so much what you do when you're together as that you are together.

Last year my cousin Mick's mother-in-law died.

The time and location of the visitation was announced and it was to be held about ninety minutes from where most of the family lived and we would have to negotiate Cincinnati rush hour traffic to get there at the appointed hour. But we did it. All four of my siblings, their spouses, and Jean and I, negotiated the traffic and undertook the inconvenience so we could be there to support our cousin's wife in the time of her loss.

When she saw us enter, she burst into tears and ran to greet and hug us. She thanked us profusely and began to introduce us to her mother's friends: "This is my family," she said. "They really rock."

Like Wind and Fire

The behavioral sciences can describe it but they have never really been able to explain it. They simply refer to it as "synergy." It is the phenomenon wherein the whole is greater than the sum of its parts. Being all together in one place seems to trigger something — something powerful and unexplainable. Luke tries to describe it but the closest he can come is a series of similes.

A sound *like* the rush of a violent wind sweeps through the house. And things *like* tongues of fire appear over the heads of those in the house. He can describe what it was like but he can't describe what it was. Whatever it was, it somehow triggers the next series of events.

Suddenly, all of those in the house were filled with the Holy Spirit, that is, the Spirit of God.

Now, I don't know about you, but I've always wondered what that would be like, to be filled with God's Holy Spirit. I've known people who claim to have had that experience and I've known people who claimed to be having that experience at the very moment I was with them.

Often, I have discovered, that what they are referring to as the "anointing of the Spirit" looks and sounds like nothing so much as a manic episode. They talk fast, they giggle, thy dance, they jump around, they run back and forth, they get ideas that they want to enact, right now, immediately. Sometimes they speak gibberish that they almost always claim is a secret religious language. And when they speak in English it is with a vocabulary and a jargon that is meaningless to everyone except their own tightly knit circle.Luke seems to have a completely different idea of what it looks like to receive God's Holy Spirit.

The followers of Jesus who were there in that house on that first Christian Pentecost day, did not run around or jump up and down. They did not laugh or giggle uncontrollably. They didn't fixate on some idea or other and not let it go. They did not speak gibberish that could not be understood. They didn't even speak in a closely guarded jargon.

In fact, they did just the opposite.

When God's Spirit entered them they suddenly began to speak in ways that *could* be understood. They began to speak not in their own religious jargon, their own comfortable words and phrases, or even in the traditional language of their culture or their faith.

No, when the received that Holy Spirit, they began to speak in ways that could be understood, understood by everyone who was standing around there at that time. They began to speak in the language of those who were trying to listen to them.

Oh, that we, the church might learn this lesson once again.

Oh, that we might cast off the jargon that we have come to love so much but which divides the world into those who speak it and those who don't, that identifies all people as insiders or outsiders, that separates us from each other when our goal should be reconciliation and reunification.

Merciful and loving God, grant again on this day of Pentecost that we might speak of your grace, your love, your mercy, your forgiveness, and your acceptance in words that can be easily understood and in ways that can be not just heard but felt and embraced, owned, and lived by all who behold them.

What's Up with This?

Of course, even when we speak the good news of God's grace in language that can be understood, not everyone will choose to understand it or accept it.

Some of the people in the crowd, that day, saw and heard it all but their response was only, "What does this mean?" Others looked for an easy and facile reason to shrug it off and dismiss it, "They're drunk."

Of course, most of us have been on the receiving end of that kind of response, haven't we?

We share our faith story with someone or we recall something we experienced at church or in a religious setting and someone hears us and responds with, "I don't get it," or, "What's up with this?" or, my favorite, "Church? You go to church? Really? Huh."

Or they take it a step further, and go on the attack, dismissing us with a generalization or a characterization. You know, like, "People who go to church are all hypocrites," or,

"I don't go to church because I don't like being judged," or, "Religion is just superstition with a different name."

Luke tells us that Peter responded to those kinds of responses.

First, he corrects the obvious inaccuracy: "They aren't drunk," he says, "because it's only nine in the morning." Yes, yes, I know that there are weaknesses in that argument but he doesn't wait around for them to be pointed out. He leaps to the offense.

These people are all Jews. So rather than argue from his own point of view as a follower of Jesus, he argues from their point of view as Jews. That is, he speaks to them in their own language! He lifts up the prophet Joel, a Hebrew prophet, and says, in effect — "Why are you surprised to see these things? Why don't you accept that these are the very things that your own prophet, Joel, predicted would happen when God's Holy Spirit was poured out upon God's people?"

Young people, old people, low people, high people, *all* people will be included. There will be visions and dreams and prophesies. The natural order of things will be turned on its head and nothing will be left untouched. Everything will be changed. Many will be panicked and many will be scared, many will feel threatened and many will feel perplexed but those who rely on God and find their strength and their courage in YHWH will be saved.

Peter's sermon goes on to tell of Jesus, his death and resurrection, his love and the salvation he makes possible through grace, and two things happen as a result of his preaching. (Notice how, in Luke's writing, things rarely happen in isolation from other things. One thing triggers another which triggers the next thing, and so on.) The first thing that happens as a result of Peter's sermon is that he and John are arrested.

The second thing that happened as a result of that sermon was that about 5,000 people believed and accepted the good news of Jesus Christ — 5,000.

I'd say that's a pretty fair trade.

If someone told me that tomorrow our church could reach 5,000 people and convince them that they are accepted and loved by God but as a result of that Stephen and I would be arrested and have to spend the night in jail, I'd say, "You gotta deal." What about you?

And that sermon, and those 5,000 people — whether that number is accurate or it is an exaggeration or it is a symbolic number — marked the birth of Christianity as a religion in its own right. It's days as a branch of Judaism were now numbered. This new faith would break the bonds of homogeneity and reach out to everyone, everywhere. Now, as those 5,000 or 500 (however many it was) souls returned to their homes and took the good news with them, it would begin to spread across the entire known world at that time.

And that community of followers of Jesus, that family of faith known as the church would be born with this manifesto, this image or one much like it, written into its very DNA:

... the Church is of God,
And will be preserved to the end of time,
For the conduct of worship
For the due administration of the sacraments,
For the maintenance of Christian fellowship and discipline,
For the edification of believers,
And for the conversion of the world.
Because all, of every age and station,
* stand in need of the means of grace which it alone supplies.*

Amen.

1. http://www.irs.gov/pub/irs-pdf/p1828.pdf
2. The United Methodist Book of Worship (Nashville, Tennessee: The United Methodist Publishing House, 1992). Fifteenth Printing: August 2005.

Trinity Sunday
John 3:1-17

Meeting Jesus

Now there was a Pharisee named Nicodemus, a leader of the Jews. He came to Jesus by night and said to him, "Rabbi, we know that you are a teacher who has come from God; for no one can do these signs that you do apart from the presence of God." Jesus answered him, "Very truly, I tell you, no one can see the kingdom of God without being born from above." Nicodemus said to him, "How can anyone be born after having grown old? Can one enter a second time into the mother's womb and be born?" Jesus answered, "Very truly, I tell you, no one can enter the kingdom of God without being born of water and Spirit. What is born of the flesh is flesh, and what is born of the Spirit is spirit. Do not be astonished that I said to you, 'You must be born from above.' The wind blows where it chooses, and you hear the sound of it, but you do not know where it comes from or where it goes. So it is with everyone who is born of the Spirit." Nicodemus said to him, "How can these things be?" Jesus answered him, "Are you a teacher of Israel, and yet you do not understand these things? 'Very truly, I tell you, we speak of what we know and testify to what we have seen; yet you do not receive our testimony. If I have told you about earthly things and you do not believe, how can you believe if I tell you about heavenly things? No one has ascended into heaven except the one who descended from heaven, the Son of Man. And just as Moses lifted up the serpent in the wilderness, so must the Son of Man be lifted up, that whoever believes in him may have eternal life. "For God so loved the world that he gave his only Son, so that everyone who believes in him may not perish but may have eternal life." Indeed, God did not send the Son into the world to condemn the world, but in order that the world might be saved through him.'"
— John 3:1-17

My friend, Phil, had his vision checked regularly when he was a kid, just like most of us Baby Boomers did. The vision tester would come to the elementary school every year and everyone would go to the nurse's office and read the eye charts.

Then he went to junior high and high school and they didn't test his vision any more. He went to college and graduated and started his career, got married, had a family and raised them and then, when he was in his mid-fifties he got Type-2 Diabetes and his physician suggested that the get his vision tested.

So he went to the optometrist in his community who gave him a battery of tests and said that he needed glasses and he should pick out some frames he liked and come back in a couple of weeks and pick them up.

A couple of weeks later he got a call that his glasses were ready and he went to the optometrist's office to get them. He tried them on and they fit well enough. The lady at the desk gave him a brief tutorial on the subject of taking care of your glasses. He paid, thanked her, and turned to leave.

He opened the door, stepped out onto the porch, looked around, seeing the world through his new glasses and he wept. "I felt like a fool, standing there crying," he said. "I was afraid someone might come out or want to go in and they'd see me there and I would be embarrassed, but I couldn't help myself. I cried because the world was so different than what I had assumed. I cried for all those years that I had been seeing things wrong — for all the things I had missed — for all the beauty that I had never noticed."

What do you call it when everything you thought you knew turns out to be wrong? An epiphany? A revelation?

Whatever you call it, that's what happened to Nicodemus that day when he met Jesus. He got new theological glasses.

He Came by Night

We are told only one specific thing about Nicodemus: "He was a Pharisee, a leader of the Jews."

Everything else we have to infer from the text.

Being a Pharisee, it's pretty safe to assume that he thought he had it all figured out. He had his systematic theology and all of his i's were dotted and his t's were crossed. He could debate unbelievers and win. He could argue the Sadducees into a corner from which they could not extract themselves. He knew scripture forward and backward and could quote it chapter and verse. He knew all of the laws of the Torah and he understood the subtle nuances that were hidden within them.

He had his bachelor's degree and his seminary degree framed and hanging on the wall of his office. He wore a clerical collar even on his day off. He liked it when people deferred to him and asked him to say the opening prayer at meetings and social events.

One did not become a Pharisee with a halfhearted commitment. To reach that level of Judaism one had to make a serious investment, do lots of work, and be totally committed. You had to take your religious life very seriously, indeed, and Nicodemus did all of that.

When it came to religion, he had it all together, and he knew that he had it all together and he liked it that everyone else knew that he had it all together.

Then, one night, he does something completely out of character: He goes, under cover of darkness, to see Jesus.

Why? Why does he go and why does he go in the dark?

Did he have some questions that he wanted to ask Jesus? Had he heard something about Jesus and the message Jesus was teaching and wanted to see for himself? Or did he see in Jesus a kindred spirit, someone who seemed to think like he thought?

His opening lines to Jesus would tend to give credence to this notion. He seems to think that Jesus has it all together, too. He may think that Jesus is Pharisee material and has come to offer him a sponsorship if he wants to join the club.

"Rabbi," he says, "we know that you are a teacher who has come from God; for no one can do these signs that you do apart from the presence of God."

A little flattery, maybe? Or is he sincere? Maybe he's just here to tell Jesus that he's a fan, that he's impressed with the work Jesus is doing. Maybe he just wants to give Jesus a pat on the back, an "attaboy" for all he is doing on behalf of the kingdom of God.

Maybe he has a question. Maybe Nicodemus has heard something that makes him question his own understanding, his own theology, his own outlook on life, and he wants to hear some more and these opening lines are meant to communicate that he intends to take whatever Jesus says to him seriously.

Whether he has come to compliment Jesus or to ask a question, he comes by night, under the cover of darkness.

His colleagues don't like Jesus and his visit would not be well taken by other Pharisees. To even hint that he might be taking Jesus seriously could bring some serious consequences down on his head. He could be excommunicated, forced to turn in his Pharisee card, simply for wanting to ask a question.

Have you ever had that experience, where you are afraid to ask a question about religion because you thought you might be judged? It's pretty common in religious circles, especially in those churches where it is believed that your very salvation is based on what you believe, that whether you go to heaven when you die depends on your forcing yourself to believe something and, if you just can't make yourself believe it, then you're going to hell.

I know that it's not uncommon for people who were raised in that kind of church to come into my office, share their doubt or their question with me, sometimes with no little fear and trepidation, and then breathe a huge sigh of relief and sometimes even come to tears because I haven't thrown them out of my office as they feared I would. I have, in fact, welcomed their doubt or their question and told them that they are not the first to confront and wrestle with that issue and I would love the opportunity to walk with them as they explored it.

If Nicodemus has come to Jesus with a question, however, he is going to be disappointed. If he has come thinking that he and Jesus are going to be buddies, friends of one mind, he's going to be frustrated.

Born Anew

Jesus' next line comes almost as an interruption: "Very truly, I tell you, no one can see the kingdom of God without being born from above." (Translations vary: born again, born anew, born from above.)

Nicodemus' translation gets it totally wrong. He is a true literalist and he wants to know how a person can be physically born a second time. Jesus explains that he is speaking metaphorically about a spiritual experience that is like being born a second time.

Nicodemus still doesn't get it. "How can these things be?" he asks.

Jesus points out that there are other dimensions of reality besides the literal, physical dimension. In particular, there is a spiritual dimension that, as a leader of the Jews and a teacher of Judaism, Nicodemus should be aware. In fact, he says, it's time to throw away those old, literalist glasses, and put on a new pair that can make you aware of the invisible, but no less real world of the spirit.

This is no easy task.

This is going to take some hard and sometimes painful work.

Just as physical birth is a difficult and painful experience, so spiritual birth can be, but it's worth it!

Do you hear what Jesus is saying? Do you hear the implications?

Experiencing the Kingdom of God as Jesus is opening it to us is not a pleasant walk through the gates of Oz. It is, rather, a birth experience. It is a spiritual experience that is going to be as full of tears and pain, of shouts of triumph, and expressions of joy and love as any physical birth has ever done. And it is to this kind of experience, this spiritual birth experience, that Jesus is inviting all of us.

Leave your religious baggage, behind. Kick your theological assumptions to the curb. Abandon all those ancient and archaic doctrines, those didactic dogmas, the oppressive rules and crushing laws, the should's and the ought's, the judgements and the adjudications.

Step away from all you have been told, take the hand of Jesus and start from the beginning with him.

That is the new birth experience he is talking about: starting all over, from the beginning, with Jesus as your guide. Not some pretend Jesus that we make up in our mind and chat with over coffee. Not some nice and ethereal Jesus whose only admonition is that we be nice like he is nice. Not some Jesus of myth and legend who is waiting to return to earth as a sword wielding judge and executioner.

No, the Jesus we are invited to walk with is the Jesus who comes to us in the gospels, the Jesus who lives and breathes in the red letters of the New Testament, the Jesus who loves and heals and teaches and frustrates and dies for those he loves in order to show them what real love looks like.

Come and walk with that Jesus and you will never see the world the same way again.

Everything You Thought You Knew

Of course, all of this hinges on our ability to admit that what we thought was so, was, in fact not so. It relies on our ability to admit that we were wrong, and that is tough.

Scientific psychology tells us that, even in the face of overwhelming evidence that we are wrong, we will go through almost unimaginable ordeals, jump through just about any hoops, undertake unbelievable difficulties to convince ourselves that we are right.

In fact, it has been proven that when people are faced with undeniable proof that they are wrong, their tendency will be to cling to their disproved ideas or perceptions even tighter than they did before.

This is called "dissonance theory" and, while it is referred to as a "theory" it is held to, now, as fact in the scientific community. (The word "theory" allows that, someday, someone may find an example that disproves the theory. None has been discovered, however, since 1957 when the theory was first identified.) If you will allow me an oversimplification, it works like this: when people discover that they are holding two mutually exclusive ideas or perceptions at the same time, they will tend to find a way to hold onto the one they've held the longest or into which they have placed the most personal investment and discard or devalue the other.

If, for instance, I have been smoking for thirty years and one day you tell me that smoking is unhealthy, I will probably try to find a reason to dismiss what you are telling me rather than quit smoking. Or, if I accept and believe your prediction that the world is going to end on July 15 and I sell my house, quit my job, and move in with you and your followers to await the end of the world then it doesn't come on July 15, on July 16 I will probably have found a reason that I can still believe in you and actually start trying to recruit other people to our little cult.[1]

All of this goes to say, simply, that it's very hard for us to admit that we're wrong. It's darned near impossible, in fact. Yet Jesus is asking us to open ourselves to that possibility, not about little, inconsequential things like which is best, Coke or Pepsi, or whether a Democrat or a Republican should be president. He's asking us to accept the possibility that we might be wrong about the very nature of the universe and our purpose within it.

He is inviting us to take everything we have thought about those things and leave them behind and to go, without that baggage, with him. His promise, if we do that, is that our lives can become more real, more authentic, fuller, better and more whole, that our lives will take on a quality that is eternal in nature, if we will come with him.

Whence Nicodemus?

So, did it work? Did Nicodemus do as Jesus suggested? Did he leave all his accumulated "stuff," his religious ideas, his rules, his judgments, his stiff, unyielding doctrines, his old spiritual baggage and follow Jesus? Or was it just too hard to admit that he was wrong?

Here's what John tells us:

Nicodemus is mentioned two more times in the fourth gospel.[2]

The first is in the seventh chapter when the Pharisees and the high priests are trying to figure out what to do about Jesus. They have sent the temple guards out to arrest him and bring him back but the guards are afraid of the crowd and they come back empty handed. When the Pharisees berate them, Nicodemus, "who was one of them" challenges them that they can't arrest him based on hearsay evidence. They really ought to go and hear him, firsthand. But they dismiss Nicodemus by reminding him that he is an outsider, a Galilean, just like Jesus and everyone knows that prophets don't come from Galilee so, any Galilean who claims to be a prophet must be a liar.

They don't seem to have the courage of their convictions, however, because they all leave and go home.

The last time that Nicodemus is mentioned is in chapter nineteen after Jesus' death on the cross. There, Joseph of Arimathea goes to Pilate to ask for Jesus' body so he can bury it in accordance with Jewish custom. Nicodemus, we are told, goes with him and brings the spices and herbs that will be used to anoint the body for burial.

Nicodemus has been changed.

No longer does he come under the cover of darkness.

No longer does he come with words of flattery.

Now, when all of Jesus' public followers have abandoned him and run away, Nicodemus and Joseph of Arimathea, two of his secret admirers, his silent followers, come forward when it is dangerous to do so, and make their love of him publicly known to the man who can do them the most harm, even Pilate, himself.

This is the invitation, the challenge and the promise that John brings to us in this story.

Behold, the light of the world who casts out darkness, who answers our questions and embraces our doubts and offers us growth, health, and fruitful living;

Behold, the bread of life, the living bread who feeds our spiritual hungers and for which we will never be hungry again;

Behold the gate through which every soul can walk who seeks to know the living God;

Behold the good shepherd who lays down his life for his sheep;

Behold the way, the truth, the life that is Jesus Christ, the Son of God.

Seek him out as did Nicodemus. Let him into your life. Come to know him intimately as he comes to you in the gospels and he will change your life if you will let it be changed. He will give it depth and breadth and a kind of authenticity that comes only from the spirit of the living God that lives in him.

Behold, he stands at the door and knocks...

Amen.

---

1. Cognitive dissonance theory was first investigated by Leon Festinger in 1957, when he and a colleague infiltrated a cult that believed that the earth was going to be destroyed by a flood. When the catastrophe did not occur at the predicted time, the really committed members, who had given up their homes and jobs to work for the cult were more likely to re-interpret the evidence to show that they were right all along and the earth was not destroyed because of the faithfulness of the cult members. Fringe members, on the other hand, were more likely to shrug it off, admit they were wrong and "put it down to experience." http://www.simplypsychology.org/cognitive-dissonance.html

2. He is not mentioned at all in the synoptic gospels.

Proper 5
Mark 3:20-35

Meet the Rose Family
(A Homily with Visual Aids)

... and the crowd came together again, so that they could not even eat. When his family heard it, they went out to restrain him, for people were saying, "He has gone out of his mind." And the scribes who came down from Jerusalem said, "He has Beelzebul, and by the ruler of the demons he casts out demons." And he called them to him, and spoke to them in parables, "How can Satan cast out Satan? If a kingdom is divided against itself, that kingdom cannot stand. And if a house is divided against itself, that house will not be able to stand. And if Satan has risen up against himself and is divided, he cannot stand, but his end has come. But no one can enter a strong man's house and plunder his property without first tying up the strong man; then indeed the house can be plundered. 'Truly I tell you, people will be forgiven for their sins and whatever blasphemies they utter; but whoever blasphemes against the Holy Spirit can never have forgiveness, but is guilty of an eternal sin' — for they had said, 'He has an unclean spirit.' Then his mother and his brothers came; and standing outside, they sent to him and called him. A crowd was sitting around him; and they said to him, 'Your mother and your brothers and sisters are outside, asking for you.' And he replied, 'Who are my mother and my brothers?' And looking at those who sat around him, he said, 'Here are my mother and my brothers! Whoever does the will of God is my brother and sister and mother.'"
— Mark 3:20-35

We begin this morning with a brief review of something most of us learned in ninth grade biology and then promptly forgot as soon as the test was over, and that is how science organizes and classifies living things.

Maybe these layers of classification will ring a bell:
- Kingdom
- Phylum
- Class
- Series
- Family
- Genus
- Species

Remember? No?

Okay, well, now you know. This is how science organizes all living things so we can see they are related to each other, when they *are* related, and how they are separated from each other when they aren't.

To start, all living things are divided into five kingdoms. I won't bore you with all their names but you know, of course, that two of them are the animal kingdom and the plant kingdom.

Kingdoms are divided into phyla (plural for phylum).

Phyla are divided into classes.

Classes are divided into series.

Series are divided into *families* and it is families that we want to talk about this morning. In fact, we are going to talk for a few minutes about one particular family — the Rosaceae (rose-ACE-ee-eye) family.

It's a big family but they are all friends of mine so I'd like to introduce you to them so you can know them a little better. Let me first introduce you to the great grandmother, the matriarch of the family.

Her name is Rose. Her family name is Rosaceae.

Would you like to meet some other members of the Rosaceae family? Their family tree has many and varied branches. For instance, here is one of her cousins:

His name is Apple. Yes, Apple is a member of the rose family.

As is... Peach.

This is cousin Plum, a close relative of Peach.

Here is cousin Pear.

Here is cousin Strawberry.

And this is a very distant cousin, his name is Almond.

They are all members of the Rosaceae family. That is to say, they are all different kinds of roses.

Weird, huh? I don't know about you, but I never thought of an apple as a kind of rose. But it is. It has some of the same DNA as a rose has. It shares its DNA with peaches, strawberries, and almonds.

But it doesn't share the same DNA with you or me.

We are members of a different kingdom. We are members of the animal kingdom.

But — and here's the fascinating part — even though we don't share DNA with roses we can still be part of the rose family. Poet Robert Frost wrote a poem about it. It's called, "The Rose Family."

> **The Rose Family**
> The rose is a rose,
> And was always a rose.
> But the theory now goes
> That the apple's a rose,
> And the pear is, and so's
> The plum, I suppose.
> The dear only knows
> What will next prove a rose.
> You, of course, are a rose —
> But were always a rose.

Robert Frost believed that you could be a member of the Rose family without becoming a plant, without giving

up your DNA and entering a new kingdom. You could be a member of the animal kingdom, as we are, and still be a rose by simply acting like a rose.
By being a beautiful person. By being kind and loving and fair and generous and good we can become members of the rose family — right next to Peach, Apple, Pear, Almond, and all the others.
And that is not unlike what Jesus is saying in the last verses of this morning's gospel lesson. You can be a member of *his* family by acting like him. You don't have to share the same blood, the same lineage, the same parents or grandparents. All you have to do to be a member of the Jesus family is to be like Jesus, act like Jesus, do what Jesus did.

A New Kind of Family

There are lots of words in the English language that are overused – arguably — no, I mean, that's one of the overused words. As in, "Orson Wells was, arguably, one of the greatest movie directors of all time."
Well, either he was or he wasn't. Take a risk, for crying out loud. Say that he was. Putting the word "arguably" in there just weakens the sentence and makes you seem like a coward who wants to hedge his bets. It's like saying that Wells may or may not have been one of the greatest movie directors of all time. What a wishy-washy sentiment. Take a stand. Give the man credit. Say that he was or say that he wasn't. Pick a position and stand by it.
Another overused word is hero.
Newscasters and writers as well as the general public use this word way too much, I think. It has almost come to mean anyone who does something extraordinary. Victims who survive some ordeal or tragedy are often praised as heroes just for surviving. People who simply help others who are in need of help are touted as heroes.

I think we need a narrower definition of what it means to be a hero, one that means more than just another role model. I like the definition that the Carnegie Hero Fund Commission uses in determining who will receive their Hero Awards each year: "A hero is someone who chooses to put themselves at mortal risk in order to save another."

It must be a choice, not just a circumstance in which they find themselves. It must be of significant risk, and it has to be to save another. Yes, I like that definition just fine.

And another word that is used too often and too broadly, especially in advertising, but in business, generally, is *family*.

Olive Garden restaurants used to have an ad campaign that said, "When you're here, you're family."

They were, they said, trying to appeal to the pathos of the traditional Italian family meal at which the family lingered and over which they talked and shared and enjoyed each other's company. But, *Business Insider* observes, "even though everyone recognizes and easily associates with the 'family' tagline, consumers have been treating Olive Garden more like a great aunt you visit on a bi-annual basis than a close relative."[1]

So they dumped that ad campaign and paid an ad agency a zillion dollars to come up with something new, fresh, and exciting, something that appeals to younger generations who have different ideas of what family may be. The new catch phrase they came up with was: "Go to Olive Garden." Overwhelming, right?

Most of us have heard or even worked for a company where the boss assures us that the company is a family. "We're just one big happy family, here." Or, when someone dies, "The entire XYZ Company family is grief stricken." Yes, that may make for a nice public image, but I always wonder, if you're all a family, can your employees call you to come and get them when their car breaks down? When their house burns down, can they stay with you until they get back on their feet? Will you come and bail them out when they've been arrested?

Because, that's what family does.

In fact, this kind of activity, this kind of behavior, this kind of relationship, according to Jesus, pretty much determines and defines what it means to be a family.

There are, it turns out, two kinds of families.

There's the kind you are related to by DNA, what we use to refer to as "blood."

And there are those you are related to by faith, love, and commitment.

Sometimes they are both the same group of people, and that's great. It's one of the sweetest things in life.

But sometimes, we are members of two families who don't even know each other: Our biological family and our faith family.

And it's all a matter of behavior.

What Strong Families Do

With just a little research of the internet, I discovered that there is no shortage of ideas and lists when it comes to defining what a strong family is. For example, one of my favorites was published by the University of Alabama on their Parenting Assistance Line website.[2]

It included these six characteristics of strong families:
1. Members spend a significant amount of time together.
2. Members communicate effectively with each other.
3. They appreciate each other and demonstrate their appreciation with words and actions.
4. They are committed to each other and seek to make decisions that will promote unity and harmony.

5. They demonstrate good coping skills, standing together in times of crisis or trouble.
6. They have shared values and convictions.

Notice that not once is DNA mentioned. That all of the family members do or do not share the same ancestors is not a contributing factor in making a strong family. That they are related by "blood" is not a factor. The important, indeed, the defining thing is how they treat each other, and how they relate to each other.

Most often, when we see a list like this, we try to figure out how we can impose these characteristics upon our biological families in order to make them stronger.

But there is another way of looking at them, too.

While these practices can make a biological family stronger, certainly, they can also be used to define what a family is. That is to say, wherever we see these six things happening in a group of people, we are, in fact, seeing a family.

Members of a church who behave like this are a family.

Members of a charitable organization, members of a social group, members of a football team, members of a committee, neighbors in an apartment building, people who work together in the same office, if they behave like this, they are, in fact, a family.

My mother used to tell a story about a little girl she met at the laundromat. Mom was there washing rugs and blankets in those big, supersize washing machines and there was a little girl there, maybe five or six years old, playing with her doll while her mother read a paperback book and waited for her wash to get done.

This little girl was bored and lonely and she struck up a conversation with my mother, a conversation that went on and on, according to mom, and covered all sorts of topics, some of which were marginally inappropriate about the machinations of the little girl's household and family life.

Eventually, as the blankets and rugs were moved to the dryers and the conversation ebbed, they both became quiet, just staring at the dryers and thinking private thoughts. Then all of a sudden, the little girl tapped my mother's arm and said, "Hey, let's be cousins."

Mom said she thought about it for a moment, "I don't know," she said. "Being a cousin is a pretty big commitment." She said it in jest but when she saw the little girl's face begin to sadden she realized that this was no light or laughing matter. So she said, "Okay," and stretched out her hand. "Put it right there, cuz."

They shook on it and became cousins. It was a decision.

We can decide to be related to Jesus, too. That's what he says.

If we act like him... well... then we're members of his family.

The family known as the Christian church.

The family of God.

Amen.

1. http://www.businessinsider.com/olive-gardens-new-tagline-is-go-to-olive-garden-2012-10#ixzz3bvWXYeSt

2. http://www.pal.ua.edu/support/stinnett.php

Proper 6
Mark 4:26-34

Little Start, Big Finish

He also said, "The kingdom of God is as if someone would scatter seed on the ground, and would sleep and rise night and day, and the seed would sprout and grow, he does not know how. The earth produces of itself, first the stalk, then the head, then the full grain in the head. But when the grain is ripe, at once he goes in with his sickle, because the harvest has come." He also said, "With what can we compare the kingdom of God, or what parable will we use for it? It is like a mustard seed, which, when sown upon the ground, is the smallest of all the seeds on earth; yet when it is sown it grows up and becomes the greatest of all shrubs, and puts forth large branches, so that the birds of the air can make nests in its shade." With many such parables he spoke the word to them, as they were able to hear it; he did not speak to them except in parables, but he explained everything in private to his disciples.
Mark 4:26-34

The kingdom of God is a pretty big deal in the Bible.

In the New Testament alone it is mentioned 72 times. In the gospels, it's the subject Jesus talks about more than any other. (The second-place winner is money.)

And yet, despite the fact that Jesus talks about it a great deal, we Christians tend to be rather unclear about what exactly is meant by this four word phrase: The kingdom of God.

There are a number of reasons for our lack of clarity.

The most obvious is that we don't understand the concept of "kingdom." It's not an idea that resides at the center of our mental map. In fact, to Americans, raised in a democratic republic, the idea of kings and kingdoms seems, at best archaic and, at worst, ludicrous to the point of being offensive. Being the subjects of another person doesn't work for us. We don't do kings and we don't do kingdoms.

Another reason we are unclear on the subject is because it has been muddied by the ongoing battle between Christian fundamentalism and the scientific community, especially those scientists who insist that fundamentalism is the only real expression of Christianity.

Fundamentalists insist that the kingdom of God is equal to heaven, that talk concerning the kingdom of God is talk about heaven and heaven is a physical, geographical place that your "soul" or "spirit" goes to after you die. Scientists who number themselves among what are called "the new atheists," — notably, Sam Harris, Richard Dawkins, Daniel Dennett, and the late Christopher Hitchens — and who require tangible, testable proof of such things, reject, out of hand, the notion of a physical, geographical place called heaven.

While these two camps wage raucous war against each other, those of us who see no conflict between faith and science are as ones crying in the wilderness that there is another way, a viable and rational way of interpreting these texts from our scriptures, a way that does not defy reason or scientific observation.

When we take all 72 of the New Testament texts together, as a whole, we see that the kingdom of God is not necessarily a physical place, neither is it solely a reality that comes to us only after we die. The kingdom of God is, if we take scripture seriously, both a present reality as well as a future one. It is qualitative as well as quantitative. It is as much about the depth of our life as the length of it; it is as much a vertical measure as it is a horizontal one. It is more about how we live now than about where we will live in the future.

And nowhere is this more evident than in the two little seed parables that Mark provides for us today.

The Mysterious Seed

When we say the word "parables" we usually think of stories, right? The Good Samaritan, the Prodigal Son — stories with character, plots, and so forth. But there is another kind of parable that is really just a cross between a simile (a comparison using like or as) and an allegory wherein the major characters or objects in the simile have a contrasting parallel in life.

These two seed parables are of this second type. They are brief simile/allegories and the first compares the kingdom of God to a seed that is sown upon the ground.

Note that Jesus rarely ever defines the kingdom of God in the gospels. He usually simply describes it. In this case beginning his description with "The kingdom of God is as if..."

"The kingdom of God is as if someone would scatter seed on the ground..." He goes on to describe the farmer going to his house after he has sown the seed then going to bed and getting up the next morning to find the seed has sprouted and grown.

Granted, he has used story teller's license to collapse time, here. Seed doesn't germinate and grow over night but that's not the point. The point is that the farmer does not concern himself with how this germination and growth happens. He is content *that* it happens. There are mysterious forces at work in this process and the farmer is perfectly fine with that. He doesn't need to know how everything works, only that it *does* work.

When the harvest time has come, the farmer doesn't say, "Whoa! I can't harvest these crops until I understand every aspect of how and why they grow the way they do." If farmers did that, we'd all starve.

Likewise, I don't have to know how my car runs to get from one place to another. All I have to know is *that* it runs and how to get it started.

I don't have to know why the value of *pi* is 3.14 in order to find the area of a circle. I just need to know *that* it is and apply it to the other numbers I have according to the formula. As far as I am concerned, it works because it works.

Our lives are filled with beautiful and wonderful mysteries that we usually accept as a marvelous thing, a gift even. Why does a certain progression of musical notes or chords give us cold chills or bring a tear to our eye? Why does the sound of a child's laughter automatically fill us with joy? Why do I breathe a little easier when I see my wife walk into the room and why do I breathe a little deeper when I first see my children from a distance?

Why am I drawn to that painting in the national gallery of art so that I can hardly walk away from it and my family has to come get me and physically pull me away? Why do I want to hear the same songs, see the same plays, hear the same stories and poems, and taste the same foods over and over again throughout my life? Why do they still give me the same measure of pleasure or joy or inspiration or unnamable whatever-it-is that they always have?

We live with mystery every day of our lives and have come to love it and accept it and even enjoy it.

Mark tells us, in this parable of Jesus, that the kingdom of God is like those other mysteries, a gift, offered to us by God, and we don't need to know the whys and wherefores of it. All we have to do is accept it and apply it to our lives just the way we accept the value of *pi* and apply it to the geometrical formulas, just the way we accept this or that piece of music and place it in on the shelf with the rest of the music that makes our lives so rich and full. Life in the kingdom of God is comfortable with the presence of awe and mystery.

And this mysterious, wonderful kingdom of God is not just someplace we go at the end of our lives. It is available to us right now if we will accept it and apply it to our daily living.

The Mustard Seed

The second allegorical simile is a more familiar one to most of us because most of us have known a grandma, an aunt, or a wife in our lives who had a necklace or bracelet with a little glass bubble on it and inside that glass bubble was a mustard seed.

"With what can we compare the kingdom of God, or what parable will we use for it?" he begins. Then he answers his own rhetorical question: "It is like a mustard seed which, when sown upon the ground, is the smallest of all the seeds on earth; yet, when it is sown it grows up and becomes the greatest of all shrubs, and puts forth large branches, so that the birds of the air can make nests in its shade."

The comparison, here, is one of size and potential.

What starts out very small can become very big, what starts out weak can become strong, what starts out insignificant can become hugely significant, what starts out unimportant can become very important indeed. And when you see this happening, Jesus says, watch out because you just may be already living in the kingdom of God.

Not every small thing becomes big but, in the kingdom of God, every small thing has the potential to become big. When you live in the kingdom, you don't dare dismiss anything or anyone regardless of their size. No person is so weak that they cannot become strong. No act is so insignificant that it can't become life-saving. No idea is so irrational that it can't lead to a problem solved.

In the kingdom there are no throw-away moments, no inconsequential conversations, no unimportant people. Every person who walks through the door is important. Every word spoken is a witness. Every life touched is a gift of God.

It's one of the many privileges and blessings of my chosen profession that I have gotten to meet and be invited into the lives of lots of people and I've been doing this profession for a lot of years, now. About the first third of those years I worked as a youth minister in the local church as well as at the district and conference levels.

Every once in a while, I'll be at annual conference, school of missions, a meeting, or event of some kind, occasionally, even at a shopping mall or grocery store, when a person will come up to me and ask if I'm Dean Feldmeyer. I'm always a little hesitant at first — you never know, right? — but I usually, eventually, confess that I am.

And then the person tells me their name and relates to me how important I was to them in their teenage years, how much they received from me, how much they learned and sometimes they even quote back to me some of the things that I said to them that they still carry around with them. Occasionally there's even a tear or two and a claim that "you changed my life," followed by a hug or a vigorous handshake.

We'll part and go our separate ways and my wife, Jean, will say, "Who was that?" And I'll have to confess, "I have no idea." And I don't. I may have known them as a teenager in the midst of dozens or even hundreds of teenagers but I have no recognition of them as an adult.

But that doesn't matter. The little seed I planted twenty or even thirty years ago, never knowing and maybe even wondering if it was doing any good at all, has grown, blossomed, and matured into something really grand and important. And here's the thing — I had no control over its growth. I didn't even know if it was growing or not. It was out of my hands. I was just sowing seeds.

This, my brothers and sisters, is life in the kingdom of God.

Little things are made big. Seemingly unimportant things are made important. The seeds which we plant sometimes grow into marvelous, active, Christian human beings.

I heard this story on National Public Radio while I was driving and I couldn't write it down so I can't vouch that every single detail is correct... but I can confidently vouch that this story, regardless of the details, is true.

Colin Atrophy Hagendorf (no, I don't know if that's his real name but I imagine it's a *nom de plume*) is a writer who was going through a creative slump a couple of years ago. One night he and a couple of friends decided to go out for pizza and as they ate they began to talk about what was the best pizza they'd ever had and what they thought was the best pizza in New York City.

Later that night Colin decided to do some internet research and see if there was a "best pizza in New York" but since there are so many pizza joints in that great city and no one had tried them all, the judgment had not been made as to which one was the best.

Colin decided to take up the challenge. He couldn't do all of New York City but he could do the island of Manhattan. He would eat a slice at every single pizza shop in Manhattan and he would write a blog about his experience. He would call the blog "Slice Harvester."

His standard for judging the best would be a pizza that he had eaten with his father when he was thirteen years old, a pizza that had grown to mythic proportions in Colin's memory to become what he had always considered the "best pizza in Manhattan." It had been on a day when his father had taken him to Greenwich Village to buy a pair of combat boots. His dad took him on this quest, he said, "because he's a *mensch*," which is a Yiddish word that literally means, a human being, but colloquially means a good person or, more often, a person with a good soul.

They were walking down the street in Greenwich Village and they passed this place. The smell was so good that they both turned around simultaneously and went back. They went into the place and bought a slice of pizza and enjoyed what they both agreed may be the best pizza they've ever eaten. This was also the time when his father showed him how to eat pizza like a New Yorker — where you fold the pizza over and eat it with one hand. "Your hands are big enough to do it right, now. You don't want people to think you're a tourist," his dad had said.

They got the combat boots, they had this really great dad and son day, years pass, Saint Mark's Pizza where they bought the perfect slice went out of business, Colin grew up, moved away from home, became a writer and decided, when he was in his early thirties, to do his "Slice Harvester" blog which happened to become very popular in the city.

Two and a half years after beginning, Colin had eaten pizza at 362 places on the island of Manhattan, blogged about every single one of them and written a book about the experience (*Slice Harvester: A Memoir in Pizza* by Colin Atrophy Hagendorf, Simon and Schuster.)

As he was writing the book he realized that of all of those slices of pizza, 362 in all, there was only one place where he and his friends went back and had a second slice so he decided this must be the best pizza in Manhattan. They just didn't want the experience to end yet, it was that good.

He called the pizza guy and told him about the book. He asked if he could come down to interview him and the guy agreed, so he went to the guy's little pizza joint. In the course of the interview he asked the guy, where he learned to make pizza. "Well," said the guy, "I actually learned from the man who lived across the street from us when I was growing up because he always made pizza for the neighborhood for important events and whatnot. I always loved that guy's pizza so I asked him to teach me."

"What was your neighbor's name?" Colin asked.

"Well," said the guy, "I don't remember but I do remember that, for a while, he had a little pizzeria in the city."

"Oh, yeah? Can you remember the name of the place?"

"Sure, it was in the East Village right next to a church — a little place called Saint Mark's Pizza."

A father, a mensch, took his son into the city to buy a pair of combat boots the kid didn't really need but, what the heck, right? They stopped for pizza and had a moment together... and a seed was planted.

A fellow made pizza for his friends and neighbors. They talked him into opening his own place where he did okay. One day a father and son came in and ordered a slice... and a seed was planted.

Do you see how it works? Maybe the seed will grow. Maybe it won't. But you plant it, either way because, hey, who knows, right? And besides, we're like farmers. Planting seeds is what we do.

What the Farmer Does

Like the farmer, we sow seeds.

When the weather is good and looks promising, we sow seeds.

When the weather is bad and washes the seeds away, we sow more seeds.

The farmer's seeds are soy beans, corn, wheat, and hay.

Ours are love, peace, kindness, joy, hope, and grace, and we sow them regardless of the weather. When the weather brings hate, we sow seeds. When the weather brings tragedy, we sow seeds. When the weather brings despair, we sow seeds. When the weather brings pain and misery, we sow seeds.

They may grow or they may not. How they grow is a mystery to us.

They may seem small and inconsequential, but that's okay. They don't have to be big, because, in God's kingdom, they all have potential — the potential to sprout, to grow, to spread out and become huge trees of grace — huge, shade giving, life-saving trees of grace.

Amen.

Proper 7
Mark 4:35-41

A Non-anxious Presence

On that day, when evening had come, he said to them, "Let us go across to the other side." And leaving the crowd behind, they took him with them in the boat, just as he was. Other boats were with him. A great gale arose, and the waves beat into the boat, so that the boat was already being swamped. But he was in the stern, asleep on the cushion; and they woke him up and said to him, "Teacher, do you not care that we are perishing?" He woke up and rebuked the wind, and said to the sea, "Peace! Be still!" Then the wind ceased, and there was a dead calm. He said to them, "Why are you afraid? Have you still no faith?" And they were filled with great awe and said to one another, "Who then is this, that even the wind and the sea obey him?"
— Mark 4:35-41

In his book, *A Failure of Nerve: Leadership in the Age of the Quick Fix*, rabbi and psychologist, Edwin Friedman, defines the effective leader as the person who is able to maintain a "non-anxious presence" in an anxious system.

He goes on to say that all systems (organizations) are, by nature, anxious. Families are anxious. Corporations are anxious. Baseball teams are anxious. Boards of directors are anxious. Armies, committees, card clubs, charities, and churches are all anxious. Especially, churches.

Their anxiety arises from the possibility that things will change, and the fear that things won't change. It arises from their lack of vision, and where there is a vision, it arises from the demands that the vision places upon them.

In all of these cases, the leader will be the person who is able to be calm in the midst of other peoples' anxiety. Unfortunately people often see this lack of anxiety on the part of the leader as a lack of caring.

This week's scripture lessons give us a perfect test of Friedman's theories. In the Old Testament lesson the Hebrew army of Saul was afraid of Goliath and their fear paralyzed them. David entered as the non-anxious presence in the midst of their cowering, paralyzing anxiety. In Mark's gospel lesson, the boat and those within it constitute an understandably anxious system. Jesus is the non-anxious, well differentiated leader whose lack of fear is mistaken for apathy by those within the system.

"Teacher," they cry out, "do you not care that we are perishing?"

In his answer to this question, Jesus reveals to us the secret of how to be that non-anxious, well differentiated leader that is so desperately needed in our current "culture of fear."

A Culture of Fear

"Do you not care that we are perishing?"

It has become *the* existential question of our age. We ask it of our leaders, our police officers, our military, our pastors, teachers, politicians and each other. We see ourselves as victims and we cry out for someone, anyone to save us. When they don't, we echo the question which the disciples asked Jesus: "Don't you care that we are perishing?" We ask it even though the assumption upon which it is based is, by and large, not true.

We are not perishing.

The crime rate is down. Joblessness is down. The stock market is higher than it has ever been. The economy is in a slow but steady recovery, the safe and reliable kind of recovery. The highways are safer, air travel is safer, our food is safer, and our medicine is safer than ever before in the history of our country. We live longer and better, more comfortably with more resources at our command than any previous generation. Thanks to modern technology, our questions are being answered and our problems are being solved at rates never dreamed of.

But none of that has changed our perception that the world is more dangerous today than it has ever been. We live in a culture of fear.

Julie Hanus, writing for the *Utne Reader* in 2009, put it this way:

> *"The dangers of modern life have a stranglehold on people's imaginations. Sociologists call the phenomenon 'risk society', describing cultures increasingly preoccupied with threats to safety, both real and perceived. And while the human species is prone to miscalculating risk, there's more at work here than frazzled modern nerves: Americans are fearful. Truly fearful. When they're asked, a majority say with certainty that the world is more dangerous than ever before. Even in the face of evidence that negates this misperception, there is no relief. We lock our doors, say our prayers, and still can't get to sleep. For the first time in history, fear is tearing society apart."*

Unscrupulous politicians and greedy capitalists find our fears — warranted or not — to be fertile ground for reaping votes and profits. By creating new laws based on zero tolerance and requiring longer prison terms for those who break them, politicians position themselves as champions of the oppressed masses who are, they insist, us. They run their campaigns based not so much on what they plan to do for the voters as on fear of what the other side may do if they are elected. Meanwhile, guns, ammunition, survivalist gear, and "home security" systems are sold faster than they can be put on the shelves. Fear is good for business.

Meanwhile, we lock ourselves in our homes or, as a nation, within our borders, paralyzed with nervous tension, unable to think or act beyond the limits of our own anxiety. On June 10, 2015, *USA Today*, ran an editorial which weighs the toll that paralyzing fear took during the, then recent, Ebola wars. They enumerated four lessons to be learned from that experience:

1. **Delay is deadly.** "By the time WHO finally declared Ebola a global public health emergency, nearly 1,000 people were dead and a chance to get ahead of the lethal virus had been squandered." World Health Organization workers were so *afraid* of "disrupting the economies of poor West African countries" that they sacrificed the public health.

2. **Calmness counts.** "When the first US Ebola patients — two missionaries stricken while working with victims in Liberia — arrived in Atlanta for treatment last August, some politicians and news media outlets seemed to be vying to see who could create the most *panic*. By October, after a tourist from Liberia was diagnosed with Ebola in Dallas, much of the country had been whipped into full freak-out mode." As we learned from Friedman, what was needed was a non-anxious presence in the midst of the anxiety and fear.

3. **Let science lead.** In this case, that non-anxious presence was best represented by the scientific minds at the Center for Disease Control. While they made some mistakes, theirs was the most measured and rational response of all who sought to stand before the cameras.

4. **Be Prepared.** We can no longer allow ourselves to be taken by surprise. Resources must be allocated to those scientific agencies and centers that are best able to respond quickly and decisively to the threats of modern disease out breaks. Policy wise, the safest place to be is squarely in the middle, a well measured distance between paralyzing fear and blind complacency.

Interestingly, this is exactly where we find Jesus in this week's gospel lection.

All in the Same Boat

This little story which Mark has given to us is not so much a story about Jesus as a parable about the nature of faith and its relationship to fear. Matthew and Luke liked it so much that they lifted it pretty much word for word and placed it in their own gospels. The only change they make is a little softening of the language when the disciples ask Jesus for his help and when Jesus turns his eye toward the disciples and their alleged lack of faith.

If we insist on taking the story literally we will find ourselves bogged down in questions about how it is possible for one to sleep in a small boat that is, literally, filling with water, why Jesus is so crabby and short with his disciples whose fear seems to be altogether reasonable, and whether, in nautical terms, a "dead calm" is really an improvement over a choppy sea.

Scholar/commentators Donahue and Harrington point out that the introductory phrase "on that day" reminds us that this story comes at the end of a day that has been filled with teaching parables. It bids us to keep our eyes and minds open for more teaching as is usually the case in Mark's gospel, the miracles are not merely demonstrations of power. They are more often demonstrations of meaning and occasions for teaching and learning.[1]

The Sea of Galilee was, at that time, about fifteen miles long and eight miles across and was notorious for its sudden and unexpected storms. Only the most adroit sailors dared go beyond where they could see the shore, so a direct crossing was always risky. At night, it bordered on foolish. Yet, this is what Jesus asks of his disciples and they comply without question.

The question does not come until they are out in the middle of the lake and a storm has appeared, a storm so violent that the boat is filling with water and in danger of sinking. And the question is, as we have said, the existential question of all who suffer and are afraid: "Don't you care that we are perishing?"

Jesus, who has been asleep on a sailor's cushion or sand bags used for ballast, on a raised platform in the back (stern) of the boat, awakes and stills the storm with a couple of words as a parent might rebuke a fussy child. "Peace. Be still."

If this is simply a miracle story, told to demonstrate the power of Jesus over nature, it might well end right here, but it does not. There is more to come, another rebuke, and this one is for the disciples.

"Why are you afraid? Have you still no faith?"

The real subjects of this story, it turns out, are faith and fear.

Again, Donahue and Harrington inform us that the adjective translated "afraid" holds several meanings, including "timid" or "fearful" and "conveys not simply fear but timidity and lack of courage." They conclude: "From the rebuke, it is clear that faith, in Mark…is not simply intellectual conviction, but also *trust* in God along with bold *action* when faced with serious threats to life and well-being."[2]

Faith = Action

The lesson taught in this simple story has been, for the most part, ignored by the church.

We Christians have been taught, and we have passed on the erroneous lesson, that faith has to do with believing things that are hard to believe, things for which there is no physical evidence, things that seem to defy objective, scientific explanation.

We have equated faith with belief. Unfaith, we have said, is the refusal to believe a thing that "should" be believed, as though we can force ourselves to believe things that, for all the world, seem to us unbelievable. This disbelief, we have been told, is nothing more than willful rebellion against God and God's word.

Mark's story of Jesus in the storm exposes this notion that faith is simply belief as utter nonsense.

For Mark, faith is not believing that a proposition about something or someone is true but acting as though it is true whether we accept it to be so, intellectually, or not. Faith is acting, risking, doing even in the face of admitted doubts. Faith is not propositional. It is not intellectual assent. Intellectual assent requires nothing of us, no risk, no courage, and no action. Faith requires action. The opposite of faith is not disbelief. The opposite of faith is paralyzing fear, the inability to move, or to act on those things that we claim to believe, in the face of danger.

I can believe that you are able to push me across Niagara Falls on a tightrope in a wheelbarrow and that belief requires nothing of me. Faith, however, requires me to actually get into the wheelbarrow.

Faith is that which allows people and institutions to be the non-anxious presence in the midst of anxiety and fear. It allows us, as individuals, to act decisively when others are frozen. It allows the church to calmly lead when the culture is mired in anxiety, or wandering aimlessly like sheep without a shepherd, or flailing about in a headlong panic.

As Janus points out in UTNE (above), fear can divide and separate us as it has our current congress. It can cause us to become so cemented into our political or theological positions that we are incapable of moving, that we become irrationally defensive, that we treat anyone who does not fall into total agreement with us as our mortal enemies.

Certainly we saw that during the "satanic panic" of the 1980's when the myth of repressed memory fueled unfounded fears of secret, satanic cults sexually abusing women and children all over the world. Scores of innocent people were convicted and imprisoned by fearful, ill-informed juries, and ignorant judges.

But reasonable fear, properly informed and considered in a rational, non-anxious way, can also bring us together.

Probably nowhere is this better illustrated than in Nina Gilden Seavey's documentary film, "A Paralyzing Fear: The Story of Polio in America."

The polio virus afflicted tens of thousands of children in the United States and around the world from about 1915 until 1952 when the number peaked at 59,000 per year in America. In 1954 Jonas Salk invented the first polio vaccine and within two years, thanks to a mass campaign to inoculate school children, the incidence had declined by 80%. Today, it has been virtually eradicated.

All this is thanks, in large part, to people working together to raise the money necessary for fighting this fearful, crippling, and often fatal disease. The "March of Dimes," created to raise money for fighting polio and treating its victims, still stands as the largest private charity in history.

While the government did little in this cause, most of the work was accomplished by private grass-roots organizations whose solidarity in purpose allowed them to overcome what many imagined to be an undefeatable foe.

The power of our foes may have decreased but the number of foes that threaten us has not decreased, since 1950 when parents in Phoenix organized the first "Mother's March on Polio" and raised $45,000 in a matter of minutes.

Disease continues to steal the lives of not just children, but many whom we love. War now seems to be our default setting. Violence in our streets is still a threat. Drug abuse still lurks in the darkness.

These foes will not be defeated by paralyzing fear and anxiety. If they can be defeated at all, they will be undone by passionate, well-ordered and committed people, led by non-anxious, faith-driven leaders.

The gospel writer Mark would agree fully with Franklin D. Roosevelt, who said, in his first inaugural address: "The only thing we have to fear is fear itself — nameless, unreasoning, unjustified terror which paralyzes needed efforts to convert retreat into advance."

May the God who armed David for the battle and, through Jesus Christ, calmed the raging storm, be in us to conquer our fears and set us on the course to a greater faith, a boundless hope, and a passionate, healing love of all human kind.

Amen.

1. Cf. the *Gospel of Mark* by John R. Donahue, S.J. and Daniel J. Harrington, S.J. (Collegeville, Minnesota: The Liturgical Press, 2002).

2. *Ibid.*

Proper 8
Mark 5:21-43

Desperation to Hope

When Jesus had crossed again in the boat to the other side, a great crowd gathered round him; and he was by the lake. Then one of the leaders of the synagogue named Jairus came and, when he saw him, fell at his feet and begged him repeatedly, "My little daughter is at the point of death. Come and lay your hands on her, so that she may be made well, and live." So he went with him. And a large crowd followed him and pressed in on him. Now there was a woman who had been suffering from hemorrhages for twelve years. She had endured much under many physicians, and had spent all that she had; and she was no better, but rather grew worse. She had heard about Jesus, and came up behind him in the crowd and touched his cloak, for she said, "If I but touch his clothes, I will be made well." Immediately her hemorrhage stopped; and she felt in her body that she was healed of her disease. Immediately aware that power had gone forth from him, Jesus turned about in the crowd and said, "Who touched my clothes?" And his disciples said to him, "You see the crowd pressing in on you; how can you say, 'Who touched me?' " He looked all round to see who had done it. But the woman, knowing what had happened to her, came in fear and trembling, fell down before him, and told him the whole truth. He said to her, "Daughter, your faith has made you well; go in peace, and be healed of your disease." While he was still speaking, some people came from the leader's house to say, "Your daughter is dead. Why trouble the teacher any further?" But overhearing what they said, Jesus said to the leader of the synagogue, "Do not fear, only believe." He allowed no one to follow him except Peter, James, and John, the brother of James. When they came to the house of the leader of the synagogue, he saw a commotion, people weeping and wailing loudly. When he had entered, he said to them, "Why do you make

a commotion and weep? The child is not dead but sleeping." And they laughed at him. *Then he put them all outside, and took the child's father and mother and those who were with him, and went in where the child was. He took her by the hand and said to her, "Talitha cum," which means, "Little girl, get up!"* And immediately the girl got up and began to walk about (she was twelve years of age). At this they were overcome with amazement. He strictly ordered them that no one should know this, and told them to give her something to eat.
— Mark 5:21-43

Roland Jaffe's brilliant and beautiful film, "The Mission" (1986) tells the true story of the Spanish Jesuit missionaries who served the indigenous (Indian) populations of Brazil, Argentina, and Paraguay during the first half of the eighteenth century.

The "Jesuit Reductions," as history has dubbed them, were mission stations created by the Jesuits to bring Christianity to the natives through education and medical service. They were independent of the Spanish government — though protected by it.

The plot of this film revolves around two particular priests. One is Father Gabriel (Jeremy Irons), a gentle, loving spirit who volunteered to take the gospel to the Guarani people. Because they had been raided, raped and murdered by Spanish slavers, the Guarani were afraid and distrustful of white people and had already killed several missionaries before Gabriel went to them. But he managed to win them over, first with his ability to play beautiful music on the flute and then through acts of love and kindness.

While Gabriel was establishing his mission, slave trader Rodrigo Mendoza (Robert De Niro), made his living kidnapping natives and selling them to nearby plantations. On one of his trips to the city, he found his fiancé and his younger, half-brother Felipe in bed together. In a blind rage, he killed Felipe in a duel.

Although he was acquitted of the killing by his friend, the governor, Mendoza spiraled into a guilty depression. Father Gabriel, who had come to the city for a meeting with the bishop visited Mendoza and challenged him to undertake a suitable penance. Mendoza accompanies the Jesuits on their return journey into the jungle, dragging a heavy bundle containing his armor and sword.

When they reached the outskirts of Guarani territory, they had to climb a treacherous cliff adjacent to a waterfall using only natural outcroppings and crude steps that had been carved into the rock by the natives. Constantly pelted by the waterfall, slipping and sliding all the way, it took every ounce of Mendoza's strength to make it to the top where he collapsed, exhausted and wanting nothing so much as just to die. When, finally, he was able to open his eyes, he saw a group of Guarani looking down at him, their leader, a man he had seen before in one of his slaving raids.

With a completely blank expression on his face, the Guarani leader took out his obsidian knife, stepped forward, leaned down over Mendoza, reached out the knife and… cut the strap that was binding the Spaniard to his armor. The camera followed the descent of Mendoza's armor and weapons, the symbols of his past, into the waterfall which had baptized him as he climbed through it and now swallowed the metal objects as they sank to the bottom of the river. Renewed and redeemed, lifted from despair and hopelessness to a new hope, a new life, by this act of grace, Mendoza accompanied Gabriel to the mission where he would become himself, a Jesuit priest and a champion of the very people he had enslaved and killed.

We cannot earn hope. We cannot create it for ourselves. We cannot build it or win it or take it.

Hope is always a gift, a gift of grace.

Jairus' Daughter

Mark illustrates this very point in his gospel through two stories of healings, both of which were, without the intervention of Jesus, hopeless. Interestingly, he sandwiches one story into another. Watch what he does:

Jairus was a leader of his church — a member of the church council, a trustee, a Sunday school teacher, and he sang tenor in the choir. He was a solid, church-going, man of God, a good man, and yet, tragedy had befallen him and his family. His little twelve-year-old daughter was sick and, in spite of everything they had tried, she was not getting any better. He feared that she was dying.

He heard of Jesus, of the healings he had performed, and he was so desperate that, even though he didn't know Jesus and has never seen any of these healings, first hand, he went to him, fell at his feet, and begged his help.

"Come lay your hands on her, so that she may be made well, and live."

Is there a desperation more intense, more acute, more profound, more desperate than that of a parent whose child is in danger? I think there is not. We will suffer any pain, endure any indignity, undergo any hardship, stand up to any power, and face down any threat to protect and save our children. We will sacrifice our future, our honor, our fortunes, even our lives in the pursuit of their wellbeing.

This week I learned that, in 2013, three out of every five, 60% of all personal bankruptcies in the United States were caused by medical bills and I thought of this story and I said, "Yeah, I get that."[1] There is nothing I wouldn't sell, hock, or leverage if it meant getting necessary health care for my children or grandchildren.

Nothing can drive us to desperation faster than our love for our family, and that's where Jairus was. He was desperate.

Jesus saw his desperation and agreed to go with him but his journey was briefly interrupted.

As they made their way to Jairus' house, a crowd formed around them, no doubt anxious to see the show that they expected would accompany the healing of the little girl. Not much different from audiences, today, no? Watch healers on TV and we see all manner of showmanship from dancing to running, screaming, shouting, and fainting. There is no subtlety in a healing service and these folks are anxious to see the fireworks.

But as they made their way through the crowd a woman snuck up behind Jesus and touched the hem of his robe.

A Brief Interruption

I say "snuck up" on purpose because that is exactly what she did. Commentators Donahue and Harrington did a wonderful job of describing the woman and her dire predicament. She had, they remind us, several things going against her.[2]

First, she was a woman and, for a holy man such as Jesus, speaking to her in public would be frowned upon and physical contact with her altogether forbidden.

Second, she was bleeding. Worse, the original language implies and most historical sources agree that the bleeding she was experiencing was somehow related to menstruation which, according to the Levitical law, would make her ritually impure. She would, in her condition, not be allowed to touch or be touched by anyone who was considered holy, as her blood would contaminate them.

The text says that she had been "suffering from hemorrhages for twelve years." This is an obvious exaggeration because constant hemorrhaging for twelve years would have killed her. It does emphasize the fact that her suffering and unpredictable bleeding had gone on for a long time.

And that is the third thing. Only the wealthy could afford physicians in those days. We are told that she has exhausted all of her resources on doctors so that means she must have been, at one time, wealthy, and now she isn't. She must have been, at one time, happily married, but because she could not become pregnant she had been dismissed or divorced by her husband. She must have been, at one time, a woman of substance, of influence, of stature and position in the community, and now she is not. She was, instead, a pariah. Her medical problems had rendered her broke, bent, humbled, alone, and unclean.

And that, too, would make her an untouchable to first-century Jews who believed that bad luck and bad circumstances were the direct result of sin. She must have, they would reason, brought this all on herself.

Not unlike Job's friends, they would have thought to themselves or maybe even said to her, *"Can papyrus grow tall where there is no marsh? Can reeds thrive without water? While still growing and uncut, they wither more quickly than grass. Such is the destiny of all who forget God; so perishes the hope of the godless"* (Job 8:11-13). In other words, her bad luck was evidence that she was guilty of something, or so they believed.

She was, in short, the kind of woman that good, decent people did not tolerate.

So, she reached out in desperation and touched the hem of Jesus' robe and she was immediately healed. Jesus felt it happen and turned and asked, "Who touched my robe?"

The disciples responded with their typical clueless, yet obvious answer: "Are you kidding? There's like a thousand people here and you want to know who touched you? Everyone touched you."

The woman, however, understood the meaning of Jesus' question and now we understand her fear and trembling. She had broken several important and dangerous taboos. She could have been dragged away and stoned for contaminating not just Jesus but every male in the crowd whom she touched. She fell at his feet — just as Jairus did — and told him the whole truth.

But Jesus responded to her — "Daughter, your faith has made you well, go in peace, and be healed of your disease."

Her past was now sealed. Her future was open. She had come in desperation, but she had left with hope. And that hope came to her as a gift of grace through Jesus Christ.

Daughter. Did you hear that?

Curious that he should use that particular word, huh? I mean, he was on his way to see another daughter, wasn't he. A girl who was, we shall discover, twelve years old, who was born the very year that this woman's bleeding began, twelve years ago.

A child who would be, by the time he arrived, dead and, consequently, just as untouchable as the woman with the bleeding disorder.

My, what a curious, fascinating, interwoven web Mark weaves with these stories.

Back to Jairus

Just as the woman was going on her way, healed of her disorder, people arrived from Jairus' house.

They brought bad news. "Your daughter is dead. You're too late. No need to trouble Jesus with it anymore."

Jesus overheard this and told Jairus, "Don't be afraid (hopeless) but believe." He then dismissed all who were there except the family of the child and his three closest friends — Peter, James, and John.

Mark described the scene as one of much weeping and wailing that implied some of those present were professional mourners who were hired by the family. Like many of our funeral customs that, when looked upon from a distance, seem silly, this one seems silly to us. But to first-century Jews, the number of mourners and the volume of their keening was a sign of how much the family loved the departed.

Jesus sent these people on their way, telling them that the child was not dead but only sleeping. This is a play on words not meant to be taken literally. The "sleep" referred to here is the same word that is associated with the "sleep of death," the eternal sleep that takes us away until the day of resurrection. The professional mourners who had seen their share of dead people simply laughed at him. They did not get it.

Jesus touched the little girl's hand, committing another scandalous *faux pas*, and told her to get up. There are about five ways to translate that phrase. My favorite is "Little lamb, arise."

And she did.

Oh, can you imagine the cheer that must have gone up at that moment? The tears of gratitude and joy that must have flowed from the eyes and down the cheeks of Jairus and his wife? How they must have fallen to their knees and embraced her so fiercely that she could not even take a breath. And then, turning to one another, embraced and wept in each other's arms, and laughed and wept again so great was their wonderful and unspeakable joy.

I have been there, brothers and sisters, in that waiting room, at that hospital bedside, when the doctor stood from his examination of the patient, closed his eyes, sighed, and then said to the parents — "She's going to be fine." I have been there when the cast was removed, or the bandage was undone, and seen the almost miraculous healing that has taken place and heard a world class surgeon, the man whose gifts and graces pieced this broken child back together, say, almost under his breath, "God is good."

I have been there when the clouds of doubt and fear have been swept away by the healing, renewing, invigorating grace of a loving God, when hopelessness and despair have been driven out and hope has been born anew.

I have been there and I can tell you that there is no joy to equal it. It is a gift greater, more beautiful, more wonderful, and more powerful than any singing of it.

The Gift of Hope

Roland Jaffe showed us, in "The Mission," and the gospel writer, Mark, showed us through these stories that hope is a product of grace and the primary function of grace is to remove barriers — barriers that separate us from each other, from God, from the creation, and from the loving, caring, giving, selves that God created us to be.

And when grace removes these barriers, hope springs forth.

In "The Mission," Rodrigo Mendoza received from the Indian leader a forgiving grace that removed the barrier of guilt, shame, and racial hatred and allowed him to become the champion of those whom he had oppressed.

In the story of the woman with the hemorrhages, Jesus removed the barriers of ancient taboo, cultural isolation, and oppressive patriarchy, not to mention the barrier of a thoughtless and callous crowd who so surrounded Jesus that she was forced to approach him on hands and knees. He removed those barriers when he allowed her to touch him and be healed and in that healing, she received new hope.

Let us not make that fundamentalist error that says this story is about the woman's physical healing, about the cessation of her bleeding only. No, this is a story about a woman not just cured, but healed in so many ways. It is the story of a woman restored, uplifted, reinvigorated, resurrected, and set free.

It is the story of a woman given hope when she was hopeless.

In the verses leading up to these stories we have seen Jesus remove the barriers of "chaotic nature, destructive demons, and debilitating illness,"[3] and now, in the story of Jairus' daughter, he removed the greatest barrier of them all, death itself.

Our separation from each other is occasioned by the death of our relationships.

Our separation from God is marked by the death of our faith.

Our separation from our potential and essential selves is sealed by the death of our acceptance of the self that God has given us to be.

Our separation from the creation is fed by the death of our ability to recognize the joy and beauty that is inherent in it.

But death is not the final word. Throughout the gospels, Jesus Christ proved that death, *even death*, need not be a barrier for us. Even death need not lead to hopelessness. Even death — any kind of death, be it physical, emotional, moral, or spiritual — need not be the ending of our lives but can, indeed, be the beginning of them.

For I am convinced, as is Paul in chapter 8 of Romans, "that neither death, nor life, nor angels, nor rulers, nor things present, nor things to come, nor powers, nor height, nor depth, nor anything else in all creation, will be able to separate us from the love of God in Christ Jesus our Lord" (vv. 38-39).

Amen.

---

1. https://www.nerdwallet.com/blog/health/2014/03/26/medical-bankruptcy/

2. John R. Donahue, S.J. and Daniel J. Harrington, S.J. *The Gospel of Mark*. Sacra Pagina series. Collegeville, Minnesota: The Liturgical Press, 2002. p. 171ff.

3. *Ibid.*, p. 179.

Proper 9
Mark 6:1-13

Like a Phoenix

He left that place and came to his home town, and his disciples followed him. On the sabbath he began to teach in the synagogue, and many who heard him were astounded. They said, "Where did this man get all this? What is this wisdom that has been given to him? What deeds of power are being done by his hands! Is not this the carpenter, the son of Mary and brother of James and Joses and Judas and Simon, and are not his sisters here with us?" And they took offence at him. Then Jesus said to them, "Prophets are not without honor, except in their hometown, and among their own kin, and in their own house." And he could do no deed of power there, except that he laid his hands on a few sick people and cured them. And he was amazed at their unbelief. Then he went about among the villages teaching. He called the twelve and began to send them out two by two, and gave them authority over the unclean spirits. He ordered them to take nothing for their journey except a staff; no bread, no bag, no money in their belts; but to wear sandals and not to put on two tunics. He said to them, "Wherever you enter a house, stay there until you leave the place. If any place will not welcome you and they refuse to hear you, as you leave, shake off the dust that is on your feet as a testimony against them." So they went out and proclaimed that all should repent. They cast out many demons, and anointed with oil many who were sick and cured them.
— Mark 6:1-13

Almost every culture has, in its foundational mythology, a Phoenix or firebird.

The one with which we westerners are most familiar is the Greek Phoenix which, like all such mythological creatures, is said to die in a burst of sparks and fire only to be born anew from its own ashes.

Because this mythological creature lives in a constant cycle of birth, death, and rebirth, the Phoenix is, in most cultures, a symbol of renewal. While early Christians rejected any literal interpretation of the Phoenix myth, they did adopt the mythic bird as a symbol for Jesus Christ, Easter, and resurrection.

It is believed that Pope Clement I adopted it as his official symbol.

Today it remains an appropriate symbol for any Christian who has had to face the reality of failure and the struggle to rise from the ashes of unrealized hopes and dreams only to begin again with renewed faith and vigor.

The Modern Phoenix

Phoenix stories abound in our culture:

Colonel Sanders, the founder of KFC, started his dream at 65 years old after receiving a social security check for only $105. Realizing that he couldn't live on that, he decided he had to come up with a plan for making money in his old age. The only marketable skill he had was frying chicken and he thought restaurant owners would love his secret recipe and use it. Their sales would increase, and he'd get a percentage of their profits. He drove around the country knocking on doors, sleeping in his car, wearing his white suit, and his idea was rejected 1,009 times before someone finally decided to try it.

Theodor "Dr. Seuss" Giesel's first book, *To Think That I Saw it on Mulberry Street* was rejected by 27 different publishers before he finally sold it.

John Grisham's first book, *A Time to Kill*, took three years to write and was rejected 28 times until he got one yes for a 5,000 copy trial run printing. Today he's sold over 250 million total copies of his books, world wide.

Steven Spielberg applied and twice was denied admission both times to the prestigious University of Southern California film school. Instead he went to Cal State University in Long Beach from which he went on to direct some of the biggest movie blockbusters in history. Now he's worth $2.7 billion and in 1994 got an honorary degree from the film school that rejected him twice.

Stephen King's first book *Carrie* was rejected thirty times

Michael Jordan was cut from his high school basketball team. He turned out to be the greatest basketball player of his generation, maybe of any generation but his most famous speech begins with these words: "I have missed more than 9,000 shots in my career. I have lost almost 300 games. On 26 occasions I have been entrusted to take the game winning shot, and I missed. I have failed over and over again in my life. And that is why I succeed."

We often make the mistake of thinking that people who are successful don't fail. The truth is that they fail, often, and they let their failures inform them but they do not let their failures define them.

Jesus as Phoenix

In this morning's gospel text, Jesus experiences failure and then offered advice to his disciples about how they should handle it when they find themselves and their message rejected.

Jesus, we are told, went to his home town of Nazareth and taught in the synagogue but these were his old neighbors and his family. They knew him when he was a snotty nosed little kid, when he had scabs on his knees, teased his little sisters, and was bossy to his little brothers. His father was the carpenter who fixed their roof and rehung their door when it came off the hinges.

They knew him and he's no big deal to them.

Sociologist Tex Sample told a story not unlike this about a softball team he played on when he was in college and working in a factory to pay his way through school. He played on the factory's team in a beer league that played in the local park in the evenings.

There was, on the team, one guy who had never caught a fly ball in his life. He was fat, uncoordinated, and not very bright. If all that wasn't bad enough, he was also kind of loud and obnoxious. No one on the team liked him very much but they had to field ten guys to have a team in the league and he was the tenth.

So on this particular night they stuck him over in right field where no ball ever went and about half way through the game, a left hander came up to bat and hit a low arching fly ball right into right field. As luck would have it, it hit right into the glove of our anti-hero. He didn't even have to move his glove. The ball just fell right into it as though pulled there by a magnet. Three outs and the good guys were up to bat.

Next inning, Tex was pitching and he and the catcher were talking, mapping out some strategy or something, and this guy was out in right field, yelling at the top of his lungs, "Hey, hit it to me. Hit it to me and I'll get ya out."

The catcher looked at Tex, shook his head, spit and said, "Listen to that idiot? He catches one ball in a whole dang season and he thinks he's somethin'. Thinks he's better'n the rest of us. That fool ain't no different from any of us. He ain't nothin'."

Tex says that was a lesson that always stuck with him. If you wanted to get along with these guys you had to keep your mouth shut and admit that you were, just like them, nothing.

That's what Jesus was confronting. He was nothing special to these people. He had nothing to say that they want to hear. They've known him too long and too well. To them, he ain't nothin'.

And because they aren't receptive, he was unable to help them. Do you hear that? He can't help them. I always thought Jesus could do anything but, apparently, he can't. He can't un-ring a bell. He can't change the past. And he can't help those who won't be helped.

Mark tells us, he is amazed at this situation. Why won't they listen to him, accept him, learn from him? He just didn't get it. But he did accept it. He did what he could — healed a couple of people — and moved on.

And when he was giving advice to his disciples about how they should go about doing ministry, he remembered this lesson and advised them accordingly:

First, travel lightly. Don't burden yourself with extra provisions trying to cover any possible eventuality. And this applies not just to your physical provisions but to your mental/emotional ones as well. Take your faith with you but don't feel like you have to pack every answer to every question in your mental suitcase. Give yourself the freedom to trust in the Lord a little bit.

Second, be a good guest. If someone invites you to stay with them, accept gracefully and stay with them. Don't be moving around trying to get a better deal, a softer bed, a bigger honorarium.

And third, if you go somewhere and they reject you or refuse to listen to you, leave. This business about shaking the dust off your shoes was an old Jewish ritual that people in those days practiced. If they went outside Israel, when they returned and crossed the border, they would turn and shake the dust off their shoes which symbolized that they were now cutting their ties with those who were not of their faith.

Jesus suggested that this was an appropriate ritual — literally or figuratively — for anyone whose ministry is rejected.

If you're a doctor and you tell your patient to stop smoking and he doesn't...

If you're a teacher and you tell your students to do their homework, and they don't...

If you're a dentist and you tell your patients to brush and floss, and they don't...

If you're a dietitian and you give your client a diet plan but she doesn't follow it...

Well, there's only so much responsibility you can take for other people, right? Kick the dust off your shoes and move on.

Tools for the Road

But it's not always that easy, is it?

We feel responsible.

It's hard to just cut your ties and move on – so God has given us four things to help us let go of failure. Actually, probably more than four, but four will do for today.

One, is grace.

We are not saved by our success rate. We are not saved by our ability to meet our goals. We are not saved by our accomplishments or our achievements.

We are saved by God's grace, God's unconditional love for us, and that is all.

If we fail, we need not worry that our value as a human being is somehow going to be lessened, that God is going to love us less, that Jesus is going to reject us at the pearly gates. Our failures do not count against us. They are, as soon as we let loose of them, part of the past that has been relegated to the dustbin of history.

We can let go of our failures because we are not saved by our success.

Two, is our capacity to learn.

We can learn from our failures.

Think of each failure as a can full of some delightful beverage that we shall call "meaning." You fail at something and there you stand with this can in your hand and you just can't bring yourself to throw it away, let it go. So what you need to do is pour the contents of that can out into another vessel- – call that vessel "memory" — and then throw the can away.

Keep the contents long enough for it to nourish you and refresh you with meaning but that is all.

Learn all you can from that failure, *then let it go.*

We can let go of our failures because we have learned from them, we have let them inform but not determine our future choices.

Three, is our capacity for story.

Each failure is a story to tell — with humor, with grace, with whit, with fun — so others can learn from it as well.

We do not have the right to horde our failures to ourselves. Our failures are gifts that have been given to us and we owe it to the world to share them with others. One of the things that separates us from other animals is our capacity to learn from the experience of others, and we dare not withhold that capacity from those who might benefit from it.

My experience can be of value to others and my failures are as much of my experience as my successes. If all I share with others are my success stories, I'm denying them a major part of the gifts that have been given to me.

We can let go of our failures because they are occasions for learning, not just for me, but for those I love as well.

And the fourth tool, the fourth gift that God has given to us in our failures, is that they teach us empathy. They teach us what other people feel like. They expand our capacity for being with and going with others who are facing uncertain roads ahead.

One of the greatest examples of this that I have ever heard was given in a TED Talk by Doctor Abraham Verghese.

TED is a nonprofit organization devoted to spreading ideas, usually in the form of short, powerful talks (eighteen minutes or less). TED began in 1984 as a conference where Technology, Entertainment and Design converged, and today covers almost all topics — from science to business to global issues — in more than 100 languages.

Over 2,000 TED talks have been archived on their web site and I encourage you to go there, from time to time, and listen to some of them. I can just about guarantee that, no matter what topic you lite upon, you will find the talks fascinating. I have never heard one that wasn't amazing.

Anyway, Dr. Verghes gave one of the most beautiful and moving TED Talks I've ever heard. It was called, "The Doctor's Touch" and he concluded his speech like this:

> *I'm an infectious disease physician, and in the early days of HIV, before we had our medications, I presided over so many scenes like this. I remember, every time I went to a patient's deathbed, whether in the hospital or at home, I remember **my sense of failure** — the feeling of I don't know what I have to say; I don't know what I can say; I don't know what I'm supposed to do. And out of that sense of failure, I remember, I would always examine the patient. I would pull down the eyelids. I would look at the tongue. I would percuss the chest. I would listen to the heart. I would feel the abdomen. I remember so many patients, their names still vivid on my tongue, their faces still so clear. I remember so many huge, hollowed out, haunted eyes staring up at me as I performed this ritual. And then the next day, I would come, and I would do it again....*
>
> *I recall one patient who was at that point no more than a skeleton encased in shrinking skin, unable to speak, his*

mouth crusted with candida that was resistant to the usual medications. When he saw me on what turned out to be his last hours on this earth, his hands moved as if in slow motion. And as I wondered what he was up to, his stick fingers made their way up to his pajama shirt, fumbling with his buttons. I realized that he was wanting to expose his wicker-basket chest to me. It was an offering, an invitation. I did not decline.

I percussed. I palpated. I listened to the chest. I think he surely must have known by then that it was vital for me just as it was necessary for him. Neither of us could skip this ritual, which had nothing to do with detecting rales in the lung, or finding the gallop rhythm of heart failure. No, this ritual was about the one message that physicians have needed to convey to their patients. Although, God knows, of late, in our hubris, we seem to have drifted away. We seem to have forgotten — as though, with the explosion of knowledge, the whole human genome mapped out at our feet, we are lulled into inattention, forgetting that the ritual is cathartic to the physician, necessary for the patient — forgetting that the ritual has meaning and a singular message to convey to the patient.

And the message, which I didn't fully understand then, even as I delivered it, and which I understand better now is this: I will always, always, always be there. I will see you through this. I will never abandon you. I will be with you through the end."

Thank you very much.[1]

Our Failures — Our Gifts

Our failures in life can be painful, even heartbreaking. No one is denying that.

But what our faith offers us is a choice. My failures can be occasional chapters in the book that is my life, or they can be the whole book. I can, by God's grace, walk through them, learn from them, and then go on to the next thing, or I can choose to put down my roots there and dwell in them.

I can ignore them or I can learn from them.

We can, with time, come to see our failures as gifts, given to us to share, along with the lessons we have learned from them, with others. Or we can simply pretend they didn't happen, learn nothing and, consequently let no one else learn anything, either.

Our failures can, if we wrap them in our faith in God and our love for each other, be amazing gifts that can heal, edify, encourage and maybe even save those who are hurting, lonely, and lost.

Amen.

---

1. http://www.ted.com/talks/abraham_verghese_a_doctor_s_touch

Proper 10
Mark 6:14-29

Promises to Keep

King Herod heard of it, for Jesus' name had become known. Some were saying, "John the Baptist has been raised from the dead; and for this reason these powers are at work in him." But others said, "It is Elijah." And others said, "It is a prophet, like one of the prophets of old." But when Herod heard of it, he said, "John, whom I beheaded, has been raised." For Herod himself had sent men who arrested John, bound him, and put him in prison on account of Herodias, his brother Philip's wife, because Herod had married her. For John had been telling Herod, "It is not lawful for you to have your brother's wife." And Herodias had a grudge against him, and wanted to kill him. But she could not, for Herod feared John, knowing that he was a righteous and holy man, and he protected him. When he heard him, he was greatly perplexed; and yet he liked to listen to him. But an opportunity came when Herod on his birthday gave a banquet for his courtiers and officers and for the leaders of Galilee. When his daughter Herodias came in and danced, she pleased Herod and his guests; and the king said to the girl, "Ask me for whatever you wish, and I will give it." And he solemnly swore to her, "Whatever you ask me, I will give you, even half of my kingdom." She went out and said to her mother, "What should I ask for?" She replied, "The head of John the Baptist." Immediately she rushed back to the king and requested, "I want you to give me at once the head of John the Baptist on a platter." The king was deeply grieved; yet out of regard for his oaths and for the guests, he did not want to refuse her. Immediately the king sent a soldier of the guard with orders to bring John's head. He went and beheaded him in the prison, brought his head on a platter, and gave it to the girl. Then the girl gave it to her mother. When his disciples heard about it, they came and took his body, and laid it in a tomb.
— Mark 6:14-29

The Days of Our Loves, Harod Style

If you like those soap opera type stories of dysfunctional families or maybe royal palace intrigue, you need look no further than the New Testament, the histories of Josephus, and the lives of the Herod Family.

Herod the Great was the patriarch of this particular and peculiar family and, as you may recall, he ruled Palestine from about 36 BCE to 4 BCE. History records that he was, quite literally, an evil genius. He was a great builder who was responsible for rebuilding the temple of Jerusalem, the fortress at Masada, and many other colossal projects. He was a savvy business man and a partner of Cleopatra in a business venture that extracted tar from the natural tar pits near the Dead Sea and used it to create a sort of primitive asphalt which they sold all over the Roman empire.

He was also criminally insane – paranoid and depressive — seeing conspiracies threatening his rule, everywhere he looked, and, as a result, was responsible for the execution of several of his wives and sons.

This is the Herod who met the three Magi and was responsible for the slaughter of the innocent children of Bethlehem shortly after the birth of Jesus.

He died in 4 BC, about the time of Jesus's birth, and, by all accounts, his death from chronic kidney disease and gangrene was long, slow, and excruciatingly painful as befits a villain of his stature but adding to his depression and paranoia.

When he finally died, his will divided his kingdom among three of his sons:

Herod Archelaus was given the territories of Samaria, Judea, and Edom but, within a very short time, proved himself to be totally incompetent and was deposed by Caesar Augustus in favor of a Roman prefect named Valerius Gratus who was replaced in 29 CE by Pontius Pilate.

Herod Philip received the "territories east of Jordan," the specific boundaries of which we do not know, today.

Herod Antipas was given the region known as Galilee where he reigned for 41 years.

At some point, around 30 CE, Herod Antipas traveled to Rome on some unspecified business and, since his half-brother, Philip, had a house there, he was invited to stay with Philip and his wife, Herodias, for the length of this stay.

It wasn't long before Antipas and Herodias found themselves drawn to each other and engaged in a torrid affair behind Philip's back and before Antipas left, he and Herodias pledged to divorce their respective spouses and marry each other. As anyone who has seen more than a few episodes of "Dallas" or "The Guiding Light" can tell you, this was a bad idea.

Antipas' wife heard about the plan and, knowing that the Herod men had, in the past, practiced a kind of divorce that involved having their wives accused of treason and then having them executed, she fled to her father, Aretas, king of Nabatea, who could not countenance such an insult to his daughter and vowed revenge against Antipas, a story that is also fascinating but need not concern us, here.

Meanwhile, Herodias declared herself divorced from Philip.

Jewish law, at this time, did not allow a woman to divorce her husband but Herodias and Philip and Antipas were all Roman citizens and Roman law did allow it. So she filed the appropriate papers and off she went to join Antipas in Galilee. (The historian, Josephus, allows that she also had another husband before Philip from which she never bothered to get divorced but, again, that does not concern us here.)

What concerns us, here, is that she married her husband's brother while her husband was still alive and, according to Jewish law, in those days, that was considered incest.

Enter, John the Baptist…

Coda: Flashback by Mark

Before we go there, we need to pause for a moment and find this story in the text so we can appreciate Mark's understanding of context.

Last week's story ended with Jesus giving his disciples instructions for going out to spread the gospel. He told them to travel light, be a good guest wherever they stayed, and, if their ministry was rejected, to shake it off and move on to someplace else.

As the disciples walked off into the sunset, Mark paused to bring us up to date on the life and ministry of John the Baptist using a literary device known as a flashback. We know it's a flashback because earlier, in chapter 1, verse 14, Mark told us that Jesus did not start his ministry until "after John was arrested."

In chapter 6 Jesus' ministry is well underway, so this is a flashback to chapter 1. As soon as the flashback ends, Jesus' disciples will return from their missionary journey and tell Jesus how it went, but while they're gone and we're waiting for them to return, Mark takes a few moments to fill in some narrative holes.

Now, Back to the Story

Up to this point John the Baptist and Herod Antipas have enjoyed a fairly tolerable, if not cordial, relationship. We are told that Herod "liked to listen to him." Some scholars believe that means that Herod listened to John from a distance and was a fan of his rhetorical skills. Others believe that he may have invited John into the palace for lively discussions about theology and Jewish law and whatnot. (They didn't have television or Facebook®, so those kinds of discussions were a popular form of entertainment among the aristocracy of that time and place.)

All that is about to end, however.

John told Herod that his marriage was an incestuous one, illegal and immoral, and he must divorce himself from Herodias and send her, and her daughter, (now, Herod's stepdaughter and niece) away.

Herodias caught wind of this and got scared. She had gone "all in" with Herod Antipas. If he kicked her out she has nowhere to go. She has burned her bridges with her ex-husband. She and her daughter will be, literally, on the street. There's also that thing that has to be in the back of her mind about the Herod men having their ex-wives executed on trumped up charges.

She went to Antipas, threw a hissy fit and told him that she was deeply offended by John the Baptist and, who does he think he is, anyway? Why, in any other country if a man — prophet or not — said something like that about the king and the queen he would be put to death, immediately. And that is what she thought should be done to the Baptist.

But Herod Antipas was reluctant to do this because he kind of liked John and he enjoyed their talks. Besides, John was a righteous and holy man who, according to Jewish law, at least, was right. So instead of having him killed, he took John into what many scholars believe was a kind of protective custody. He was under arrest but probably treated pretty well, considering. This way Herod and John could continue to have their talks and play chess or whatever.

But Herodias didn't like her husband talking to John, at all, so she held a grudge and bid her time.

A few weeks later, Herod threw himself a big birthday party. He invited all his courtiers, officers, the satraps, governors, and other high ranking officials of Galilee and, in the Roman tradition, it was a multi-day, drunken, blowout of a party.

At one point during the party his stepdaughter/niece, who was named Herodias, after her mother, came in and danced for Herod and his guests.

She was not named Salome, by the way.

Coda: Whence "Salome"?

Salome was the name given to her by the Jewish Roman historian, Josephus who wrote his *Antiquities of the Jews* in about 93-94 CE. By the mid to late 1800's the story of the palace intrigue that led to John the Baptist's execution was the stuff of much fascination for artists and writers in Europe.

It was in1891 while visiting France and experimenting with the styles of the symbolist and decadent movements that Oscar Wilde wrote his play, *Salome* which was loosely based on the biblical account. It was also Wilde's version of the events which dubbed Salome's dance the "Dance of the Seven Veils," a kind of seductive striptease.

In the play, however, it was Salome herself (not her mother) who called for John's execution because she was angry with him for being immune to her seductive charms and, in return for her duplicity and cruelty, Herod had her killed by his bodyguard.

As I said, it was "loosely" based on the biblical account.[1]

Now Back to the Story, Again…

Whether Herod was simply an enthusiastic patron of the art of dance, or a drunken letch being seduced by his teenage stepdaughter, we cannot know, but he offered to reward the girl for her wonderful dance and told her she could name her own prize, anything she wanted, up to half of his kingdom.

Confused and a little taken aback by the generosity of Herod's offer, she ran to her mother and asked for her advice and, here, Herodias saw her chance and took it.

"What shall I ask for?" the girl asked.

Mother replied, "The head of John the Baptist."

The daughter wasted not a minute in returning to Herod. "I want you to give me, at once, the head of John the Baptist on a platter."

Mark told us that Herod was "deeply grieved yet, out of regard for his oaths and his guests, he did not want to refuse her." He sent a member of his bodyguard with orders to see to the execution and when the head of the Baptist was brought forth, the girl received it without a qualm or a hesitation and, in turn, gave it to her mother.

Mark concluded the story by telling us that, when John's disciples heard about his death they came, took his body, and laid it in a tomb.

The Story, Then

The story of the death of John the Baptist achieved several things for Mark and his immediate audience who were very probably dealing with a cult of John the Baptist who were still, even thirty years after his death, revering and even worshiping him as the messiah.

First it shows us that Jesus was *not* the reincarnation of John the Baptist or Elijah or one of the other Old Testament prophets. He was a unique individual as was his cousin, John the Baptist.

Second, it shows that John the Baptist was not raised from the dead as some were, no doubt, claiming was the case. Here, in the story, Mark puts that claim right out on the table. Herod says, along with some unnamed others, that they think Jesus may be John the Baptist raised from the dead.

With this story, Mark laid that notion to rest.

Here, Mark made it clear that John was a prophet of God who was martyred for speaking truth to power as was sometimes the case with prophets. *The Lives of the Prophets*, an apocryphal book written at some time during the life of Jesus, said that many of the ancient prophets died this kind of death.

Isaiah of Jerusalem was, according to legend, sawed in half for confronting King Manasseh.

Jeremiah was allegedly stoned to death for speaking an unpopular truth to the ancient Egyptians.

Ezekiel was supposedly "killed by the Chaldeans."

Micah was ordered executed by King Jehoram.

Amos was said to have been tortured by Amaziah the high priest and murdered by Amaziah's son.

Zechariah Ben Jehoiada was beheaded beside the altar in the temple by order of King Jehoash.

It didn't stop there, in the Old Testament; by the time Mark wrote his gospel it is likely that Paul had been beheaded, Peter had been crucified, James the brother of Jesus, had been thrown from the wall of the temple, then stoned and beaten to death, James the son of Zebedee had been executed by Herod Agrippa, Andrew was crucified in Greece, and Stephen had been stoned to death, all for speaking truth to power.

John the Baptist was one in the endless line of splendor that was the prophetic tradition.

But he was not the messiah. And that was, to a great degree, Mark's point in telling us this story. But he had another point as well.

The Story, Now

For us, the story of John the Baptist's death is the story of two men and two promises.

Herod Antipas was the king whose worldly power was the power of life and death over others. He had the power to take a life but he was powerless to save the life of an innocent man whose only crime was telling the truth.

Desperate, afraid, and exposed, Herod was willing to sacrifice the life of another, an innocent, in order to maintain his honor, his prestige, and his power.

John the Baptist, on the other hand, was the innocent, the exact opposite of Herod, who was willing to sacrifice himself in order to maintain God's word and God's will for the sake of all the people.

Herod was the king whose promise became his prison, who found himself bound hand and foot by his own words, unable to act except in the cause of self-preservation.

John was the pauper, the desert hermit, dressed in animal skins, who was so detached from his sense of self that he was able to speak truth to power with no thought of the personal consequence.

Herod was a symbol of the old way, the empire who ruled by the power of violence, oppression, and despair.

John was the harbinger of the one who was coming, the one who would announce the dawn of a new kingdom, a kingdom of love, and light, and life, even Jesus, the messiah, the Christ, the Son of the living God, in whose name we are this day come together, and whose name we have taken upon ourselves when we choose to be called Christian.

Amen.

---

1. Because it was illegal, during his lifetime, for biblical characters to be portrayed on stage, Wilde never saw *Salome* performed. Richard Strauss did bases his opera, however, upon a German translation of Wilde's play. A movie version of the play, directed by Al Pacino, was completed in 2013 but released theatrically only in the United Kingdom. DVD versions are available but not widely.

Proper 11
Mark 6:30-34, 53-56

Missional Discontinuity

The apostles gathered around Jesus, and told him all that they had done and taught. He said to them, "Come away to a deserted place all by yourselves and rest a while." For many were coming and going, and they had no leisure even to eat. And they went away in the boat to a deserted place by themselves. Now many saw them going and recognized them, and they hurried there on foot from all the towns and arrived ahead of them. As he went ashore, he saw a great crowd; and he had compassion for them, because they were like sheep without a shepherd; and he began to teach them many things... When they had crossed over, they came to land at Gennesaret and moored the boat. When they got out of the boat, people at once recognized him, and rushed about that whole region and began to bring the sick on mats to wherever they heard he was. And wherever he went, into villages or cities or farms, they laid the sick in the market-places, and begged him that they might touch even the fringe of his cloak; and all who touched it were healed.
— Mark 6:30-34, 53-56

What is it with Americans and work?

We work, on average, 1,836 hours a year, more than just about anyone else in the industrialized world, and we take less vacation. 42% of working Americans don't take any vacation at all and, of those who do, 61% report that they were working when they should have been playing![1]

Paid time off makes up, on average, 7% of an American workers' compensation package but most workers don't collect all that they are entitled to. In fact, according to *Fortune* magazine, the average American worker leaves about five paid days off per year unclaimed. If the company isn't buying back that unpaid leave, then workers who work on days when they should be off are, in fact, paying their employers for the privilege of working on those days.[2]

For all kinds of reasons, some of which we will talk about in a few minutes, many Americans don't like to take time off.

I am not one of those.

I love vacation and I take every moment I can get. I like vacations on the beach and I like vacations in the mountains. I like adventure vacations that involve seeing new places and doing new things. I like going back to old, familiar, and comfortable places to do the same old things that we do every time we go there. Yeah, I even like those "stay-cations" where you do local things that you never get a chance to do, like go to the Underground Railroad Museum, the Art Museum, or the Aquarium. I don't think I ever met a vacation I didn't like.

And, according to the experts who measure and keep track of such things that makes me healthier, smarter, happier and more productive than those who martyr themselves on the altar of their job.[3]

Another minister I know who likes vacations nearly as much as I do calls her vacations "missional discontinuity." We go away, she says, so we can come back. We discontinue so we can continue better.

I wonder if Jesus had something like that in mind when he bade his disciples, "Come away to a deserted place by yourselves and rest a while."

News Fatigue

I'm something of a news junkie and, I have to tell you this was a pretty stressful week for people like me.

Greece was going bankrupt. United Airlines could not get its planes into the air due to a computer glitch. Another computer glitch had shut down the Wall Street Journal's home page and a third had managed to close the New York Stock Exchange. People were actually wondering aloud if this could be that big cyber-attack that computer literate people had been warning us about.

These stock market problems were especially troubling because they came at a time when China's market was teetering on the edge of a cataclysmic sell-off that could rock the economy of the entire planet. ("Could" being the operative word, here.)

The deadline for sealing a deal with Iran was creeping up and every time Secretary of State Kerry thought they were about to achieve an agreement, Iran wanted to change the rules — or something. I don't really understand what's going on over there.

Meanwhile, in Hollywood, Bill Cosby was back in the spotlight after a recently revealed admission that he had purchased drugs he planned to use to molest women. Down in South Carolina the state legislature was voting on whether or not to take down the Confederate flag, and ESPN announced that Caitlyn Jenner would be receiving the Arthur Ashe Courage Award at the ESPYS. Oh, and Donald Trump, apparently, won't be happy until he's offended every single person in the northern hemisphere.

My diet soft drinks are, allegedly, making me fat, and they just discovered that my ibuprofen is going to give me a stroke or a heart attack.

On the local front, the All Star Game was going to be played in Cincinnati and if you live within a thousand miles of the "Queen City," you were expected to be all aquiver with anticipation as were all of our local news media.

And if all these things aren't stressful enough, in and of themselves...

Every time I read a news story on my computer home page, when I get to the bottom of the story there's a place for "Comments." It's not enough to just read the story or listen to the story. No, now we're expected to have an opinion about what we just read or heard — right now — immediately.

It's not enough to be informed. We're also supposed to be outraged, indignant, excited, keyed up, worked up, fired up, overwrought, and generally all astir over everything we see.

What we really are is overwhelmed and, when we add that to the normal stresses of work, family and community life, we are also exhausted.

What we need is a vacation. We need a vacation from the constant barrage of news that assaults us when we turn on our computers, when we eat our lunch at McDonalds, when we get our hair cut, and even when we stand in line at the bank.

We need a vacation from the culture's insistence that we have an opinion about everything.

But we are Americans and, as noted, we aren't real comfortable taking time off. Some of us are afraid we won't have a job when we get back. Some companies offer time off but then create a culture of overwork so people are afraid to take their time off because doing so may put them at the bottom of the promotion list. Others say that the amount of work they have to do before they can leave and after they get back just isn't worth the time off for vacation.

And there's the mixed messages that our culture is sending us.

Again, *Fortune* magazine's article, which ran in May of 2016, insisted on the importance of vacations for the company as well as the workers, and how necessary it is that everyone take all of their allotted vacation time. They pointed out that people who do are generally more productive at and positive about their jobs. Companies who encourage people to take all of their allotted vacation time tend to be more profitable and successful.[4] But, on the other hand, Republican presidential candidate Jeb Bush, seemed to be saying just the opposite: "We have to be a lot more productive, workforce participation has to rise from its all-time modern lows. It means that *people need to work longer hours*." (emphasis added)[5]

As Christians, however, our concern is not so much what Jeb Bush says or what *Fortune* magazine says as what Jesus says.

What Jesus Says

In this Sunday's gospel lection, Mark told us of two stories where Jesus and his disciples were overwhelmed by the volume of work and the depth of need that had been set before them.

In the first story, the disciples returned from their missionary journey upon which Jesus dispatched them in verses 6-13. They were excited and eager to share with Jesus all that had happened to them but there were so many people with so many needs coming to them for help that they did not have time to even eat their lunch, much less talk about what happened last week.

So Jesus bid them "Come away to a deserted place all by yourselves and rest a while." But their escape plan didn't work. People saw them crossing the lake in their boat and ran around the shore to be there before the boat arrived.

When Jesus came ashore, he saw that these people were "like sheep without a shepherd" and he had pity on them and taught them many things.

The lectionary skips the story of the feeding of the 5,000 and the story of Jesus walking on water and calming the sea. That will come another week.

Instead, we jump to the end of that story and an event that was nearly identical to the one we have just seen. The disciples and Jesus escaped the crowd only to be confronted by them and even more when they reached their destination across the lake. This time Jesus responded by healing people.

Let's be clear that the needs of the vast crowds of anonymous people are very real and very urgent. And there are lots of them. Quite specifically, Mark identifies two kinds of needs that are as real and urgent today as they were at that time.

In the first story Jesus sees that the people are like sheep without a shepherd. That is, they are leaderless, unfocused, unorganized, at odds as to what to do next and liable to get themselves into trouble if someone doesn't help them pretty quickly. Jesus sees that need and decides to help them and the way he helps them is by teaching them.

He does not take them by the hand and say, "Oh, you poor, poor thing." He does not empathize with their plight or enable them in their ignorance and lack of direction. He doesn't invite them to tea or tell them to "turn it over to the Lord." He teaches them.

The first need is for teaching, and it still is.

I truly believe that one of our greatest needs as a people and as the church is for education, and honest education at that. First, we need to teach and be taught an unsanitized, historical account of who we have been and from where we have come.

We need to know the truth about our past. We need to have our stories painted in vividly honest colors and we need to see our ancestors as they were, "warts and all." We need to know about our mistakes as well as our triumphs, our moral lapses as well as our moral victories, our bad choices as well as our good ones, the things for which we can be proud and the things for which we need to apologize.

And we need to teach an unsanitized Jesus. We need to give ourselves the freedom to learn and to teach that what Jesus offers is a radical, counter-countercultural, alternative to what the world offers. We need to know and teach that when Jesus tells us to love our enemies, sell what we have and give it to the poor, and take up our cross and follow him, he is not speaking in meaningless metaphors and ambiguous aphorisms. He is serious. He is giving us the very essence of what it means to be one of his disciples.

Only then, when we are well supplied with honesty and a sense of calling, can we begin to take care of the second need that Mark identifies in those who sought out Jesus — the need for healing.

We tend to focus on the physical healings that are identified here but there are many kinds of blindness, many kinds of deafness, and many kinds of brokenness, my friends, and I am convinced that the cure for many if not most of these ills can be found in Jesus Christ.

Jesus Christ can cure our broken relationships if we will place them before him. Jesus Christ can heal the blindness of prejudice, bigotry, and enmity if we will but submit to his prescription. Jesus Christ can open our ears to love, joy, mercy, and peace if we will but listen to him with our whole being.

The need for teaching and the need for healing are as real and as urgent, as authentic and as pressing now as they were 2,000 years ago, brothers and sisters. Jesus is calling us to be the teachers and the healers, now just as he called his disciples to do then.

But we must be careful in this worthy and holy pursuit. These same passages that call us to service also provide that there are times when we must take leave of service, even important and urgent service, in order to meet another set of needs — our own.

Too Busy to Eat

I have spoken before of the theological significance of that warning they give in commercial airplanes as you are taxiing out to the runway. They tell you how to operate the oxygen mask should it be necessary to use it and then they say, "If you are traveling with a small child or a person with disabilities put your own mask on first, and then help those seated near you." In other words, you are not going to be of any help to anyone if you are flopping around, gasping due to an oxygen deficiency of your own.

Jesus says the same thing but in a different way:

The opening sentence of this story is the first time where the disciples are referred to as "apostles." This is appropriate, as an apostle is one who has been sent and they are just returning from the mission field into which Jesus sent them. But being sent out comes at a price, does it not? Yes, they are excited to share their experiences but that same excitement can, if they aren't careful, lead to burnout.

It is exciting to be needed. It is flattering when people come to us and ask for our expertise, our knowledge, our abilities. And we genuinely want to help, if we can, for helping others in need is almost the very definition of what it means to be Christian.

But the disciples were so busy helping others that they could not find the opportunity or the leisure to even have a meal together. They were sacrificing their own nutrition and their own health in their service to others. They were setting themselves up to be classic cases of burnout.

They had either forgotten or never learned the lesson of the oil lamp: It is not the wick that burns but the oil. As long as there is fuel in the lamp the wick will last a very long time. But when the fuel runs out the wick begins to burn and the fire soon goes out.

We who are commissioned to teach and spread the good news of God in Jesus Christ and to heal the brokenness of the world, cannot afford the luxury of burning out.

The story speaks of food and eating but, again, we need more kinds of nourishment than that which is supplied by fishes and loaves alone.

We need mental nourishment, the kind that comes from taking the time to learn something new about ourselves, about our religious faith, about the world around us.

We need the emotional nourishment that we get from spending time, structured or unstructured, with our friends and our families, playing, talking, listening, laughing, and just basking in the warmth of their love.

We need the spiritual nourishment that comes from prayer, meditation, corporate worship, and the study of scripture.

An old friend of mine, an avid fisherman, had a bumper sticker on his truck that said, "If you're too busy to fish, you're too busy." In the stories we heard the gospel writer, Mark, made the same case for eating. If you're too busy to eat, you're too busy. And, by extension, he made this point as well:

If, in our ministry to others, we find ourselves too busy to learn, too busy to love, too busy to worship, too busy to pray, well, then we're just too busy. And it may just be time to go "away to a deserted place… and rest."

Amen.

1. http://www.news-star.com/article/20150703/BUSINESS/307039981/-1/op
http://fortune.com/2015/05/01/paid-time-off-vacation/

2. *Ibid.*

3. *Ibid.*

4. http://www.csmonitor.com/USA/Politics/Decoder/2015/0709/Did-Jeb-Bush-really-say-Americans-need-to-work-more-hours

Proper 12
John 6:1-21

More than Enough

A Stewardship of Resources

After this Jesus went to the other side of the Sea of Galilee, also called the Sea of Tiberias. A large crowd kept following him, because they saw the signs that he was doing for the sick. Jesus went up the mountain and sat down there with his disciples. Now the Passover, the festival of the Jews, was near. When he looked up and saw a large crowd coming towards him, Jesus said to Philip, "Where are we to buy bread for these people to eat?" He said this to test him, for he himself knew what he was going to do. Philip answered him, "Six months' wages would not buy enough bread for each of them to get a little." One of his disciples, Andrew, Simon Peter's brother, said to him, "There is a boy here who has five barley loaves and two fish. But what are they among so many people?" Jesus said, "Make the people sit down." Now there was a great deal of grass in the place; so they sat down, about five thousand in all. Then Jesus took the loaves, and when he had given thanks, he distributed them to those who were seated; so also the fish, as much as they wanted. When they were satisfied, he told his disciples, "Gather up the fragments left over, so that nothing may be lost." So they gathered them up, and from the fragments of the five barley loaves, left by those who had eaten, they filled twelve baskets. When the people saw the sign that he had done, they began to say, "This is indeed the prophet who is to come into the world." When Jesus realized that they were about to come and take him by force to make him king, he withdrew again to the mountain by himself. When evening came, his disciples went down to the lake, got into a boat, and started across the lake to Capernaum. It was now dark, and Jesus had not yet come to them.

The lake became rough because a strong wind was blowing. When they had rowed about three or four miles, they saw Jesus walking on the lake and coming near the boat, and they were terrified. But he said to them, "It is I; do not be afraid." Then they wanted to take him into the boat, and immediately the boat reached the land toward which they were going.
— John 6:1-21

Forty percent of all the food that is produced in the United States is thrown away.

That's about twenty pounds per person per month, a total of about 33 million tons or $165 billion worth of edible, nutritious food per year. Discarded food is the second highest component of landfills in this country that as it decays, becomes a significant contributor to methane emissions.[1]

Worldwide, western, industrialized countries waste about 30% of all produced food, an annual total of about 220 million tons, an amount roughly equal to the entire annual food output of sub-Saharan Africa.[2]

How does all this food get wasted? A few years ago the National Resource Defense Council, an organization that tracks food usage and waste "from farm to fork" (as they say) came up with this data:

1) **Farming:** Roughly 7% of the produce that's grown in the United States simply gets stranded on fields each year. Some growers plant more crops than there's demand for, to hedge against disease and weather. Some produce goes unpicked because it's ugly and people won't buy it. Food-safety scares account for some food going unpicked and fluctuating immigration laws can also create shortages of farmworkers, which can leave food unpicked.

2) **Post-harvest and packing:** After crops are harvested, farmers tend to cull produce to make sure it meets minimum standards for size, color, and weight. One farmer estimated that fewer than half the vegetables he grows actually leave

his farm and that 75% of those that are culled before sale are edible and nutritious.

3) **Processing and distribution:** Technical malfunctions in processing and refrigeration can sometimes cause food to sit too long at improper temperatures and spoil. Stores often reject entire shipments because of damage to a few items — and it's often difficult for distributors to find a new taker.

(Some years ago I was working at a food bank in Lima, Ohio, when an entire truck load of canned kumquats was delivered to the food bank for that very reason. Kumquats!)

4) **Retail and grocery stores**: The USDA estimates that supermarkets toss out $15 billion worth of unsold fruits and vegetables each year because they've begun to ripen or a new shipment has come in to replace what's already on the shelves.

Supermarkets throw out, on average, $2,300 worth of food each day because the products have neared their expiration date. Yet most of it is still edible. In many states, it's perfectly legal to sell food past its expiration date but most stores would just prefer not to, and many customers won't buy it. Most stores, in fact, pull items two to three days before the sell-by date.

5) **Food service and restaurants**: On average, diners leave about 17% of their meals on their plates. The reason — gigantic portions. Restaurants also have to keep more food than they need on hand so they can meet all of the demands. Ten percent of all food cooked in fast food restaurants is thrown away before it is served because of time limits. (McDonalds throws away fries at the seven-minute mark.)

6) **Households:** American families throw out between 14% and 25% of the food and beverages they buy. This can cost the average family from $1,365 to $2,275 annually. A big factor here is that food has become so cheap and readily available that people feel like it's no big deal if some of it gets tossed. There's always plenty more where that came

from. The report also notes there's a great deal of confusion around expiration labels, which often prompt people to throw out food prematurely.

7) **Disposal:** Only 3% of thrown-out food in the United States is composted. Most ends up in landfills, where they decompose and release methane, a powerful heat-trapping greenhouse gas. In fact, about 23% of US methane emissions come from landfill food. Composting or even technologies to capture methane could reduce that.

Americans today waste 50% more food than they did in the 1970s.[3]

The United Nations Resource Defense Council collected data for the United States, Canada, Australia, and New Zealand and discovered that, in these four countries, only 48% of all fruits and vegetables produced are actually eaten. Only half of all seafood that makes it to land ever makes it to the table. Only 38% of grain products, 22% of meat, and 20% of milk that is produced for consumption is ever actually consumed.

All of this waste, all of this food gone uneaten, and yet…

More than a third — 34.9% — of American adults (78.6 million souls) are obese. These people suffer from high blood pressure, heart disease, stroke, type 2 diabetes, and certain types of cancer at rates far higher than the rest of the population. The estimated annual medical cost of obesity in the US was $147 billion in 2008 US dollars; the medical costs for people who are obese were $1,429 higher than those of normal weight.

We are throwing away and we are eating more food than any population in 200,000 years of human history. And we are doing it while 795 million people, 11% of the world's population, do not have enough food to lead a healthy, active life.

Forty-five percent of all deaths of children under five years of age, approximately 3.1 million per year are caused by poor nutrition; 25% of the world's children are stunted in growth because they don't have enough of the right foods to eat.[4]

Brothers and sisters, when 11% of the people are suffering from debilitating hunger while we throw away 40% of the edible food, something is seriously wrong. We need to be better stewards of our resources. We need to discover a new morality of nutrition, a new food ethic for our country. And, as we search to do so, we could do worse than to start with scripture and the story that the gospel writer, John, presents to us, today.

Feeding 5,000

The story of the "Feeding of the 5,000" is that rare story that appears in all four of the gospels. In fact, it is the *only* miracle story, aside from the resurrection, that appears in Matthew, Mark, Luke, and John. And, as with the resurrection story, there are differences in each telling.

It is also the only story that is told six times in the gospels, appearing twice in Matthew and twice in Mark. Most scholars, today, allow that even though Matthew and Mark render the stories as "The Feeding of the 5,000" and "The Feeding of the 4,000" they are, essentially, the same story. Luke and John apparently believed that to be the case and omitted the "Feeding of the 4,000" as unnecessarily redundant.

Since this story is one of only two that appears in all of the gospels, and since it is the only story in the Bible that is repeated six times, it must be important, so let's take a few moments to unpack it, shall we? In particular, let's spend some time exploring the things John has decided to tell differently from the other gospel writers.

I mean, he must have had a purpose for changing the story from how it originally came to him in Mark's gospel, so, as we go, let's explore what that purpose might be.

As in all of the gospel accounts, in John's gospel the disciples and Jesus were overwhelmed by the crowds of people who were coming to them, mostly because they had seen or heard of sick people being healed and they either had friends and relatives who they wanted Jesus to heal, or they just wanted to see the show.

And, as in the other gospels, Jesus and the disciples tried to get away from the crowd for some rest and relaxation but their efforts were thwarted. A large crowd had either already gathered at their destination or, as in John, a large crowd could be seen coming toward them.

In Mark, the first gospel to tell this story, Jesus responded to the crowd by teaching them.

Matthew and Luke, who received the story from Mark, changed that. Instead of teaching, in those two later gospels, Jesus healed many of the people in the crowd.

John leaped over this healing versus teaching so he could get straight to the theological issues.

There is one question that drives this story for John: "How are we going to feed these people?"

That's the existential question, the practical question, yes. There is, before us, the very real and necessary question of resources. How are we going to feed all these people?

In the synoptic gospels (Matthew, Mark, Luke) it is the disciples who asked this question of Jesus.

In John, what had been a practical question now became a theological one. Here, Jesus was doing the asking and he had picked one particular disciple to ask the question to: Philip.

"Philip, where are we going to buy bread to feed all these people?" And this, John tells us, was not a real, practical question but a rhetorical one. It was asked not because they needed a plan and Philip was the most likely disciple to have one. It was not asked because Philip had a Garmin that could tell them how to get to Walmart. It was not asked because

Philip was familiar with the territory and knew where the bread store was. It was asked not because Jesus was truly flummoxed about what to do. It wasn't even asked because it was somehow the responsibility of Jesus and the twelve to feed all these people. In reality, it was not.

It was a rhetorical question, asked, as all rhetorical questions are always asked, as a teaching tool. Jesus knew what he was about to do and he wanted to see if Philip could figure it out. What he was asking Philip was, "Do you know who I am and what I am capable of doing?"

Alas, Philip didn't get it. He gave a practical answer to a rhetorical question. There weren't any stores to send the people to and, even if there was, Jesus and the twelve don't have enough money to make the necessary purchase. Couldn't be done. There were insufficient resources. It would take a miracle.

Sound familiar?

You'd think that, after 2,000 years, we would know the answer to this question was simply, "With you, Jesus, anything is possible." But we still haven't learned it, have we? We still find ourselves, whenever we are confronted with a big problem, counting our resources and declaring the situation hopeless.

Oh, we can't possible put a new roof on the building. It's way too expensive.

We can't open our Vacation Bible School to the community. We don't have enough teachers and volunteers.

We can't support a missionary. We don't have enough money.

We can't teach a Sunday school class. We're too old and we don't have the energy.

You don't need to spend too much time around a bunch of Christians to hear Philip's lament being spoken over and over again — *we don't have enough* — money, energy, time, volunteers, chairs, space, insurance, knowledge, or experience. We are very good at counting, cataloguing, and announcing the things that we don't have enough of.

Philip is us, isn't he? He had forgotten to whom he was speaking. He was so focused on his lack of resources that he could not see the abundance of resources that Jesus brought to any situation. And that, my friends, is all too often, us.

Fishes and Loaves

Andrew enters the story and what follows only happens in John's gospel. (In the synoptic gospels it's the disciples, themselves, who have the loaves and fishes.) I can see Andrew sort of sidling up to Jesus and Philip, not wanting to interrupt, but certain that he had information that Jesus would want to know.

"Uh, excuse me. I hate to interrupt but there's a kid over here who says he has a couple of smoked herring and about five loaves of whole grain bread." Then I always imagine that he kinda rolls his eyes as if to say, "Yeah, I know it isn't enough to do any good, but whataya gonna do, right?"

And we have to wonder about the boy, don't we? Many scholars believe that the word "boy" is a Greek word that carries the implication of a servant or slave. In fact, the "boy" in question may not have been a child, but an adult servant or slave who had been sent to the market and was on his way back when he stopped for a few minutes to take in this Jesus phenomenon and who, naively offered the meager bag of food he was taking to his master to help feed 5,000 people.

If this was the case then he and Andrew were showing a little more faith and insight than Philip but only a little more. Andrew supposed that it was possible that the fishes and loaves might be put to use, but he hedged his bets by adding a "but probably not" to his offer.

The resources were insufficient, we will not have enough.

But Jesus stepped in and made insufficient resources sufficient… in fact, more than sufficient. And he did it with a three-step program. Watch what he says and does because in his actions we find a prescription for the church. *Here's what you do when the resources you have don't seem sufficient:*

First, he had everyone sit down.

That is, he imposed a sense of calm order upon the situation. Calm and order may be two of the greatest gifts we can bring to any situation where the existing resources seem insufficient for that task that is at hand.

Do you remember that delightfully funny and insightful book from a few years ago called, *The Hitchhiker's Guide to the Galaxy*? And do you remember what it said was on the cover of the Hitchhiker's Guide?

"Don't panic!" The author, Douglas Adams, then went on to tell us: "It is said that despite its many glaring (and occasionally fatal) inaccuracies, the *Hitchhiker's Guide to the Galaxy* itself had outsold the *Encyclopedia Galactica* because it was slightly cheaper, and because it had the words "DON'T PANIC" in large, friendly letters on the cover."

Serious science fiction author Arthur Clark said that Douglas Adams's use of that phrase, "Don't panic," was the best advice that anyone could ever give to humanity.

Second, he gave thanks for, that is, he turned the food over to God.

Were it left up to Andrew or the unnamed boy, or Philip, or even Jesus, for that matter it would have been impossible. None of them, alone, could have fed all those people. Jesus agreed with this because he asked for God's help by giving thanks for the bread and, in doing so, he offered up the bread to God to be used for God's purposes.

Rarely are our resources sufficient, in and of themselves, for the tasks that have been placed before us. Rarely does what we bring to the table fill the need all by itself. We need more. We need God's help.

We understand this when the subject is one of healing. We are all aware that the healing of even the smallest wound or cut is a miracle. I cut my finger, I pour some peroxide on it, slap on a Band-Aid®, and in a couple of days, when I take the Band-Aid off, the cut has healed. The cells have regenerated and knit themselves back together and my finger looks as though there was never a cut there at all.

No matter how much money I have, how much political power I wield, how many degrees I have managed to earn, how much wealth I have managed to accumulate, or how much my friends love me, I cannot will this kind of healing to happen. It is outside of my control. I do not have sufficient resources to force it to happen.

I am dependent upon a source of resources that is outside of my control.

I call that source, God. And so does Jesus. By blessing the bread and fish, he is turning them over to God and asking God to make them sufficient.

Third, he took the resources that he had just blessed and he gave them away.

No forms filled out in triplicate.

No regimen of questions to insure that only those who are "truly needy" get the goodies.

No drug tests, no snotty attitude, no lectures, no tsk-tsk'ing, no counting to make sure no one comes back for seconds. He simply took what he had and gave it away — not reluctantly, not carefully, not even responsibly, but generously.

Note, if you will, please, the phrase which John has added to this story that none of the others includes: "…he distributed them to those who were seated; also the fish, *as much as they wanted.*"

How often do we want to be generous, seek to be generous, try to be generous but find ourselves tempering and mitigating our generosity with qualifications:

"I want to be generous but I don't want to be taken for a fool." Or, "I'm willing to be generous but I won't be taken advantage of." Or, as I once heard a man say, "I consider myself a generous person but I'm also a careful and responsible one."

Well, friends, I don't see Jesus, the one we call our Lord, being all that careful, or cautious, or even responsible, here. Those will come in a moment. Right here, however, he's just being generous. Lavishly, generous. Wastefully, generous.

More than Enough

Then, after everyone had all they wanted to eat, when they were "satisfied," (From the root word "sate" which means to fill up so that no more is wanted.) Jesus gave his disciples another task, one that he did not speak in the other gospels. In the synoptic gospels, the leftovers were mentioned almost as an afterthought, a footnote to the story.

But for John, it was part of the very center of the narrative.

Jesus said to them, "Gather up the fragments left over, so that nothing may be lost." And, we are told, the leftovers filled twelve baskets.

Large baskets or little ones, the children in my church ask. It doesn't matter. Twelve is a symbolic number that just means "many." There were lots of leftovers.

After Jesus had imposed calm and order, after he had turned over the meager resources he had to God, after he had generously given away the resources at his disposal, why then God simply took over and made those resources sufficient and then some. God made them more than enough.

And Jesus' response to God's generosity was to see to it that nothing was wasted.

When God gives us more than we need, brothers and sisters, we have a responsibility. If we have more clothing, more food, more money, more of anything than we need, John shows us in this story that we have a responsibility to see to it that none of it goes to waste.

Remember when you were a kid and your parents admonished you to clean your plate and not waste food because there were children starving in other parts of the world? Remember that?

Turns out, they were correct.

Who knew, right?

Amen.

1. http://www.npr.org/2012/11/23/165774988/npr-the-ugly-truth-about-food-waste-in-america

2. http://www.worldfooddayusa.org/food_waste_the_facts

3. http://www.washingtonpost.com/blogs/wonkblog/wp/2012/08/22/how-food-actually-gets-wasted-in-the-united-states/

4. https://www.wfp.org/hunger/stats

Proper 13
Mark 2:23–3:6

Never on Sunday

One sabbath he was going through the cornfields; and as they made their way his disciples began to pluck heads of grain. The Pharisees said to him, "Look, why are they doing what is not lawful on the sabbath?" And he said to them, "Have you never read what David did when he and his companions were hungry and in need of food? He entered the house of God, when Abiathar was high priest, and ate the bread of the presence, which it is not lawful for any but the priests to eat, and he gave some to his companions." Then he said to them, "The sabbath was made for humankind, and not humankind for the sabbath; so the Son of Man is lord even of the sabbath."

Again he entered the synagogue, and a man was there who had a withered hand. They watched him to see whether he would cure him on the sabbath, so that they might accuse him. And he said to the man who had the withered hand, "Come forward." Then he said to them, "Is it lawful to do good or to do harm on the sabbath, to save life or to kill?" But they were silent. He looked around at them with anger; he was grieved at their hardness of heart and said to the man, "Stretch out your hand." He stretched it out, and his hand was restored. The Pharisees went out and immediately conspired with the Herodians against him, how to destroy him.

— Mark 2:23—3:6

There are not ten commandments; there are only nine.

That other one, the one about resting and not working on the Sabbath, that's really just a suggestion. No one, not even the most observant Christians — with the possible exception of Hobby Lobby and Chick-fil-a — take it all that seriously, and even they simply close their businesses. Whether or not they actually rest and remember, as the commandment requires, is anyone's guess.

Business Insider lists In-and-Out Burger, Marriott, and Forever 21 as three of the top seventeen most religious companies in the country but they all pretty much ignore the fourth commandment, as does Walmart who claims to run their company based on the principles of Christian servant leadership.[1]

And all this is so if you interpret "Sabbath" as Sunday. If you interpret it as sundown Friday through sundown on Saturday, as did the ancient Hebrews, first-century Jews, and the early, primitive Christian church, then just about everyone except the Jews and the Seventh Day Adventists have tossed out that "Never on Sunday" commandment.

It wasn't always that way, though.

There was a time, about 2,000 years ago when people, religious people, Jewish people took that commandment very seriously, indeed. In fact, they took it so seriously that they spent a great deal of time and effort trying to determine what constituted "work" so they could be sure that they didn't do it on the Sabbath.

Let's take a minute and talk about that, shall we?

Remembering and Resting[2]

Shabbat, the Hebrew word for what we call Sabbath, is the only religious rite that is established and proscribed in the Ten Commandments. It is therefore the most important of all Jewish religious observances.

We pretty much take for granted the five-day work week, but that is a relatively new thing. In the times of the Bible there was no such thing as a weekend. The rich took time off whenever they liked, the poor, never. There was nothing to protect them from an employer who would make them work from dusk to dawn, seven days a week.

This commandment created one 24-hour period out of the week, from dusk on Friday to dusk on Saturday, as a time set aside for two things:

It was a time for 1) resting, and 2) remembering.

Resting meant not working, but it didn't mean not working at all. Some types of work were permitted, such as those actions required for religious rituals or preparing to eat a meal that had been cooked beforehand. Work that contributed to the remembrance part of the day was also allowed – playing music, reading aloud, recitation, those kinds of things.

Work that wasn't allowed was called, in Hebrew, *melachah,* which generally refers to the kind of "work that is creative, or that exercises control or dominion over your environment." Also prohibited would be any work that achieved the same purpose. Specifically, the early rabbis listed 39 tasks that were prohibited along with any other task which was undertaken for the same purpose. (see Appendix on p. 139)

These tasks are, basically, the kinds of work that was undertaken to build the temple and, since the building of the temple was always halted for *Shabbat*, it seemed appropriate that that kind of work should always be halted for this sacred and holy day of the week.

Also, the time of resting wasn't supposed to be spent taking naps but "remembering the significance of *Shabbat*, both as a commemoration of creation and as a commemoration of our freedom from slavery in Egypt." Singing songs and recounting these important stories in poetry and literature were a big part of the Sabbath observance.

A thousand years later, in the first century CE, things had gotten a little twisted.

The law as it comes to us in the Torah was given to human beings by God to draw us closer to God and to each other. Its purpose was not arbitrary or accidental. It was meant to help us create a community of faith and justice where people live together in peace.

But human nature being what it is, this same law that was given as a gift to make for a just, peaceful, fair, equitable, and faithful society had been seized and reshaped by the religious/political leaders of that very same community and turned into something that does the opposite of what it was intended to do.

It was dividing and separating the people into subgroupings based on ethnicity, economics, place of birth, education, and religious practices. And it was separating people from YHWH.

This was all being done in two ways represented by the two stories that the gospel writer, Mark, placed before us this morning.

An Illegal Nosh

In the first story, the law had been perverted into a club for beating people into submission and a trap for ensnaring heterodoxy (unorthodox ideas).

Jesus and his disciples were walking through a field of grain on the Sabbath and as they walked some of the disciples absentmindedly stripped some grains off of the stalks, rolled them in their hands to remove the chaff, and popped them into their mouths to eat. It was a common way to snack in the fields. What, in Yiddish, is called a "nosh" (snack).

Some Pharisees who apparently were walking with them for reasons not explained, pounced on this violation of the *Shabbat* rules. Harvesting was not allowed on the Sabbath and this picking and eating of grain constituted harvesting. Gotcha!

They asked Jesus why his followers were willfully breaking the laws about Sabbath observation, a violation which, if they really wanted to push it, was punishable by death (Exodus 31:14).

Jesus answered a question with a question: Haven't you read in the sacred texts how David was starving and broke into the temple and tricked the priest into giving him some sacred bread that only the priests could lawfully eat?

Before we go on, let's be honest. Mark had just massacred the story that was recounted in 1 Samuel 21. The parallels between David and Jesus were, pretty much, nonexistent. In the David story there was no mention of hunger, he didn't have any companions with him, he did not enter the house of God, and the high priest is Ahimelech, not Abiathar, and neither David nor his companions actually ate the sacred bread.

Mark had rewritten the story to make a Christian point about the Sabbath and, by inference, the law in general. *The law was made to serve human beings. Human beings were not made to serve the law.* If David could violate a silly law with impunity in order to serve a greater good, then certainly Jesus should be able to do so as well.

The law was given to draw us closer to each other in community and closer to God. When it ceases to do that it has failed in its purpose and a new law needs to be written.

A Withered Hand

The second story is more serious and more important than the first because it showed the law being perverted in such a way as to dismiss and even condone callousness and cruelty.

Jesus and the disciples entered the local synagogue, which is primarily a place of learning and a sort of local substitute for the temple as a place to worship. Inside the synagogue, he met a man with a withered hand; probably, the language tells us, a malady from birth.

Mark built tension by shifting the camera's eye from Jesus to his audience, the religious leaders who were watching to see if he healed the man which, they believe, would be a violation of the Sabbath prohibition against working.

Note that neither of these two stories was about whether or not the Sabbath should be kept sacred. That was a given with which Jesus heartily agreed. These stories are about the definition of work, of *melachah,* and what work was allowed and what was not.

So Jesus invited the man with the withered hand to come forward and he asked the Pharisees, "Is it lawful to do good or to do harm on the Sabbath, to save life or to kill?" This was not a rhetorical question and the answer would have been obvious to even the most casually observant Jew of that or this time.

Any Sabbath law can be broken to save a life. This applied not just to human life but to animal life as well. The most common example being, if you were walking along the road on the Sabbath and you saw an ox stuck in the mud would it be lawful to do the work necessary to free the ox? The answer is always "yes" because you would be working to save a life. Even if you're not sure whether or not you're actually saving the life, if you have reason to believe that you were, that is enough.

And, of course, it is not lawful to do harm, to ever murder another human being (cf. commandment number six), on the Sabbath or any other time. It is unlawful to slaughter or butcher an animal for food on the Sabbath. Jesus was pushing those laws and commandments even further. They had, up to now, been applied to action, and he applied them to inaction as well. What he seemed to be saying was that it was just as wrong to not do good, when you can do good, as it was to do evil.

All this was just too complicated and difficult for the Pharisees who believe that the guy's hand would still be withered on Monday so why not just wait until then so you don't have to break *Shabbat*? But rather than making that argument, they said nothing and Jesus, for the first and only time, shows that he is angry toward them. These religious leaders who had perverted the law in such a horrible way that it made it illegal to heal a suffering soul disgusted him.

With that, he healed the man's hand and the Pharisees left and began to conspire with the Herodians, a political group for whom they, heretofore, have had no use. Their conspiracy was to kill Jesus, not because he was wrong but because he embarrassed them and showed them to be the hardhearted prigs that they truly were.

Sacred Cows Make the Best Burgers

The point of these two stories has very little to do with the Sabbath. They are not really about the definition of work and what is allowed on the Sabbath and what is not. To let them drag us into that discussion would be very like committing the same mistake that the Pharisees make.

The point of the stories, the issue at hand is, in fact, "sacred cows" and idolatry.

The legal prohibition against working on the Sabbath is, simply, an easy springboard into this broader concern: When have we allowed the sacred cows of our religion to become twisted and perverted so that they become clubs for beating people into submission or traps for ensnaring those who dare to question popular orthodoxy?

Likewise, and more importantly, *when have we allowed our sacred cows, our rituals, our traditions, our doctrines, and our dogmas, to become idols that we worship, that rob us of our compassion, our kindness, our sense of charity, and our love of our fellow human beings?*

When, in other words, do we allow our sacred cows to become more important to us than our relationships with each other and the Lord, and what do we do about them when they do?

Up to this point I have dealt with this subject in a nice, safe, general way that is sure to offend no one. After all, this passage couldn't possibly be about *my* sacred cows, right? *My* sacred cows are never idolatrous. It's *other people's* sacred cows he was talking about.

Up to now it's just been a broad, general kind of thing, safe and inoffensive.

But...

I'm going to conclude this sermon with a few specific sacred cows that I believe are currently running loose in our own Christian churches, sacred cows that need to be rethought and possibly re-contextualized. Perhaps some need sent to the slaughterhouse before they become idols that we place at the center of our worship instead of the God who comes to us in Jesus Christ:

The Bible

The first is the Bible.

After a lifetime of study and more than thirty years of professional ministry, I have come to believe that the biggest sacred cow, one that has already been placed on the altar and worshiped as an idol in many churches, is the Bible.

We have forgotten that the Bible is not God. It is a sign that points us toward God but it is not God. It is a story that tells us about the relationships of ancient cultures with God, but it is not God. It is an account of the good news of God's love and mercy and acceptance... but it is not God.

We must free ourselves from that idolatry that is biblical literalism. We must, if we are going to grow in our faith, stop worshiping the Bible, and start wrestling with it, struggling with it, contending with it, discussing it, and, at the very least, studying it. Just reading it and expecting it to work some kind of magic in our lives is not enough.

It's neither a talisman nor a grimoire.³ It carries with it no magical power or magical knowledge. It is, above all else, a story that needs to be studied, compared, and applied for it to have any meaning or power at all.

Religious Language

The second sacred cow is religious language.

We do love our religious language, do we not? The words and phrases we learned as children and youth gave us comfort and understanding throughout our lives and we loathe to let go of them. But, there are cases where we must let them go if we are going to effectively carry out the great commandment that Jesus gave to us: "Go and make disciples."

It's time to purge phrases like "Holy Ghost" and "blood of the Lamb" from our religious vocabularies. They are symbols that no longer speak to anyone outside of the closed circle that is fundamentalist Christianity. They smack of superstition and are most often met with repulsion from those both in and outside of the church.

How can we invite a new Christians into our church and then sing a hymn like "There is a Fountain Filled with Blood" and "Are You Washed in the Blood?" and not expect them to be at least a little confused if not totally grossed out?

The phrase "born again" is utterly without meaning to those who aren't and to many who are but don't realize it.

Words like "holiness" may have had meaning 200 years ago when John and Charles Wesley called their first prayer groups "holy clubs" but today that phrase smacks of religious zealotry and fanaticism.

If our missionaries of the past 200 years have taught us nothing else, it is that, when we go into the mission field we must be able to speak the language of those to whom we are taking the gospel. If we go speaking only our own language we will usually accomplish little more than offending and alienating the very people with whom we are trying to establish a bond.

Religious Capitalism

I'm a big fan of economic capitalism. I believe that when it is done right, honest competition in the marketplace can create some pretty great things like America. For all its shortcomings, this is a pretty great place to live. Sometimes I wonder at all the marvelous and amazing things that are available to us in this country and how lucky I am to have been born here. I mean, it's really pretty awesome, and much of it has come my way because of capitalism.

But I also believe that capitalism must be left at the door of the church.

The church of Jesus Christ is not a capitalistic institution.

It is not a store where we go to purchase spiritual food to get us through the rest of the week. It is not a store where the customer is always right, and to which our only responsibility is to show up, get what we want or need, pay the check, and leave until we need something else.

Even a cursory examination of the New Testament shows this to be the case. We are a community of faith, a family, a body where every organ and limb has an important task to do and without which the body is incomplete. We do not function to make a profit, but to serve a God. The pastor is not the CEO, but the pastor, a word that comes from the Latin root meaning *shepherd*. The members are neither the customers nor the employees but members of the church, even as the hand and the foot and the eyes are members of the body.

Those are just three institutional sacred cows. There are local ones as well (chicken barbecues, vacation Bible schools, Sunday school classes, meetings, reports, and so on) and even personal ones (the pew I sit in, my favorite hymn, the time the worship service begins, what kind of clothes people in church should wear, and so on).

You can always identify them by asking one simple question: "Is this bringing people closer to God and each other, or is it dividing, separating, estranging people and, in general, creating problems for our life together, but we keep on doing it, anyway, because we always have?"

Robert Kriegel, in his book *Sacred Cows Make the Best Burgers,* says, "Individuals and organizations that are good react quickly to change. Individuals and organizations that are great create change."

Rethinking and, sometimes, letting go of sacred cows requires change, change with which all of us are sometimes uncomfortable. Jesus didn't call his followers to be comfortable. He didn't just react to change. He created it, not for its own sake, but for the sake of the world, the world which he loved and for which he died.

In the light of that great sacrifice, it seems little enough to ask for us to occasionally loosen our grip on just a few of our sacred cows, whether they are doctrinal, ecclesiastical, traditional, institutional or personal.

After all, sacred cows really do make the best burgers.

Amen.

---

1. http://www.businessinsider.com/17-big-companies-that-are-intensely-religious-2012-1 and http://religion.blogs.cnn.com/2012/07/24/7-religious-companies-besides-chick-fil-a/

2. A mythical book of magic spells.

Proper 14
John 6:35, 41-51

Metaphors Be with You

Jesus said to them, "I am the bread of life. Whoever comes to me will never be hungry, and whoever believes in me will never be thirsty... Then the Jews began to complain about him because he said, "I am the bread that came down from heaven." They were saying, "Is not this Jesus, the son of Joseph, whose father and mother we know? How can he now say, 'I have come down from heaven'?" Jesus answered them, "Do not complain among yourselves. No one can come to me unless drawn by the Father who sent me; and I will raise that person up on the last day. It is written in the prophets, 'And they shall all be taught by God.' Everyone who has heard and learned from the Father comes to me. Not that anyone has seen the Father except the one who is from God; he has seen the Father. Very truly, I tell you, whoever believes has eternal life. I am the bread of life. Your ancestors ate the manna in the wilderness, and they died. This is the bread that comes down from heaven, so that one may eat of it and not die. I am the living bread that came down from heaven. Whoever eats of this bread will live forever; and the bread that I will give for the life of the world is my flesh."
— John 6:35, 41-51

His name was John Davis, he was my neighbor, and he was a peculiar person. Don't get me wrong. I liked him but even his wife said John was an "acquired taste." I sometimes think that, had he been born thirty or forty years later, he would have been correctly diagnosed as having Asperger's Syndrome or some other condition associated with the higher functioning end of the Autism spectrum.

He was a gifted man, to be sure, a tool designer and metallurgist who worked for a big corporation, very smart and very detail oriented. He loved machines and discovering how they worked. He invited me, one time, to accompany him to hydroplane races on the Ohio River and he spent the day down on the dock talking to the mechanics and the drivers about the boats, their design, the engines, and any other technical detail he could pull from them.

We went to a tractor pull and he spent most of the time lecturing me on the different kinds of tractors and their engines and what had been done to them to give them more power.

His wife said that he loved to visit museums but he could not leave until he had read every single placard and plaque in the place and explained to her what they said. He was especially delighted when he caught one in an error. He was the neighborhood fix-it guy with a basement workshop full of old radio tubes and switches and small, old electrical appliances from which he cannibalized parts for the ones he was fixing.

He never allowed a mechanic to touch his car and insisted on doing all the engine repairs himself.

That man loved machines.

People, not so much.

He had a hard time making eye contact and he had a habit of standing too close when he talked to people and then mumbling what he said until it was nearly indecipherable. He hated parties and any situation where he was forced to talk to people he didn't know. At neighborhood functions he could usually be found on the perimeter, nervously clearing his throat and scratching his forearm. Or he would find someone who was interested in machines, corner them and mumble to them incessantly until they could figure out how to escape.

He was a literalist in every sense of the word. He took everything anyone said to him literally. He didn't understand or use figures of speech. When someone spoke a metaphor in his presence I could see the wheels turning in John's brain as he deconstructed the mental image and, after a few moments, came to the conclusion that this was not a thing to be taken literally. Then, sometimes, he would chuckle to himself and repeat the metaphor a few times, often to the person who said it but more often just to himself.

I never realized how much of our normal speech is made up of metaphors until I moved in next to John and had to try to communicate with him. Eventually, I learned to stay away from figures of speech, hyperbole, or metaphors of any kind when talking to him. Other folks, who were not forewarned and just talking to John as they might talk to anyone, often found themselves trying to explain a common, harmless metaphor or, even worse, listening to John deconstruct and explain it.

They might mention, for instance, that they had just been to a "coin laundry" and after a few brief moments of cogitation, John, snickering, would ask them if their coins were clean now. Several times.

One time he and I were sweating profusely in the summer heat as he helped me do some things that would keep my miserable, old car running a few more months. His wife, Ginny, brought out a couple of tall glasses of lemonade and reminded us that as hot as it was it would be prudent for us drink lots of liquids.

When she was gone John looked at me, rolled his eyes, and asked, in all seriousness, "What, did she think we were going to drink, solids?" Then he shook his head. Women. Whata ya gonna do, right?

When his daughter said she'd be back in a few minutes he insisted on knowing how many a few was. When she said she'd see him later he wanted to know what time later came at. He refused to countenance phrases like "awhile" or "some" or "a bunch." He insisted on concrete numbers.

At first. I found all of these quirks of John's to be ridiculous and just plain rude. After a couple of years of knowing him, however, I began to learn that John wasn't being intentionally difficult. That was just his way. It was the way his brain worked. He was simply incapable of deciphering the thousands of symbols and metaphors we use in everyday language, and the effort required to do so often left him exhausted and confused and impatient.

As you can imagine, John had no patience with anything so frivolous and inexact as religion with its symbols and rituals and its multitude of metaphors.

Today's gospel lesson, for instance, would have sent him running to the door, shaking his head, clearing his throat and scratching his arm in a flurry of confusion and frustration.

There's Bread, and then There's Bread

I sometimes think that the gospel's author, who is also named John, selected a whole bunch of metaphors, symbols, parables, stories, quotations, that sort of thing, and dumped them all into a giant blender, turn it on "frappe" for a few seconds and then dumped them all out onto paper. That is, for me, a pretty good description of chapter six of the Gospel according to John.

It all starts with the feeding of the 5,000 with five loaves of bread and two fishes. Then comes the crossing of the Sea of Galilee at night, when Jesus decides to walk across the water instead of riding in the boat. When the crowd wakes up and sees that Jesus is gone, they run to the other side of the lake so they can ask him some questions, the most pressing of which is, "What must we do to do God's will?" Jesus answers that believing in him, the one who is sent by God, is God's will. They respond that they need a sign of some kind to know he's authentic. After all, Moses gave the people manna (bread) to eat and they followed him. What can you give us? they ask.

Jesus answers with a metaphor.

First, he says, it wasn't Moses who gave you that bread, it was God. And now God is giving you a new kind of bread the bread which can save the world, the bread that is life itself.

The people respond by saying that this new kind of bread sounds pretty good. Give us some of this bread of life, they say. Where is it? And Jesus responds," It is I! I am the bread that comes from heaven (like the manna did) and who comes to me shall never hunger or thirst anymore."

That's verse 35 which the lectionary gives us as an introduction to today's reading. It's a metaphor!

Unfortunately there were some John Davises in the audience that day. The author calls them "the Jews" but he obviously doesn't mean every Jew in the audience. More likely, he's talking about the Jewish leaders, the scribes, the Sadducees, and the Pharisees, the priests, people like that. And they are as incapable as John Davis of deciphering a metaphor.

In verses 38 which the lectionary skips over, Jesus has also said that "I have come down from heaven, not to do my own will, but the will of him who sent me." And it's that line that the Jewish leaders latch onto. The obvious metaphor, here, is Jesus comparing himself to the manna which saved the Jews when Moses was leading them out of the wilderness. Remember? They were starving and it fell from the sky every night and was collected and eaten the next day, thus saving their lives.

But these learned scholars and leaders don't get the metaphor. They take it literally. "Wait a minute," they all say.

"We know this guy. We know his mother and father and we knew him when he was a snotty nosed little kid and when he was a wild teenager and we know for a fact that he didn't come from heaven. Please! Don't make me laugh."

So, in verses 43-47 Jesus gets literal. He says what he means and he makes four important points:

1) Stop whining and complaining about the things I'm saying when you obviously don't get it;

2) Stop worrying that I'm drawing people away from the one true religion. Anyone who follows me has been selected by God to follow me and they will be raised up on the last day; and

3) This is all according to scripture. Check out Isaiah 54:13 and Jeremiah 31:34; and

4) I have seen God, the Father and whoever believes in me and what I have to say has (not will have, but HAS) eternal life.

Then, in verse 48, Jesus jumps right back on the metaphor again. "I am the bread of life." The manna which fell from heaven saved your ancestors' lives but that was a temporary save. They all died anyway. I am talking about the new bread, the next bread, the final bread. You eat this bread and you never die. And that next bread that I'm talking about? It's me.

I am the new manna that has come down from heaven to save the people. Whoever eats this bread will live forever. And be clear, the bread that I will give so the world can be saved is not just an idea. It's not just a new philosophy or a new perspective on life. It's not a saying you can put on a bumper sticker or a bromide you can cross-stitch and frame and hang on the wall. It's not a secret formula for better living or a three or five or twelve point plan.

No, it's my flesh. My body. My very life.

I will give it freely and, if you accept it, your life will be eternal.

After the Bread Is Eaten

It is unfortunate that for much of Christian history we have turned this vital and powerful movement, this dynamic, transformative, spiritual experience that is the encounter with Jesus Christ into a list of rules no different, in character, from those found in the Torah.

You must believe this.
You must do that.
You may not, under any circumstances, do this.
You must not believe that.
Virgin birth? Yes or no!
Miracles? Believe or don't believe?
What about tobacco and alcohol?
Conservative or Liberal.

Christianity in so many of our churches and communities is not so much about being struck by the grace of God as it comes to us in Jesus Christ as it is about lining up and fitting in with everyone else in the church – doing the right things, wearing the right clothing, observing the right rules, and believing the right doctrines.

If you don't line up perfectly with this group, go across the street. There's another group there and maybe you'll line up with them.

This is especially tragic when we realize that this is nothing like what Jesus talked about us doing and being. For Jesus it wasn't about rules, it was about relationships. For Jesus, it wasn't about outward appearances, it was about inward transformation. For Jesus, it wasn't about obeying the rules, it was about living the gospel

It was and is about being struck by the reality that Jesus lived and loved and taught and healed and forgave so that we might know what it looks like to live a full, robust, authentic, eternal life. And he voluntarily went to the cross, and gave his life, so that we might come to know on that third day after, that death has no power over us, that our lives are gifts of God to take up and lay down as we choose.

I don't suppose we can talk about bread as a metaphor without thinking of Holy Communion and the bread and wine that are part of that powerful, metaphorical ritual that is to the Body of Christ what the spine is to our bodies. For it is in that symbolic meal that we find ourselves living out our faith as more than a list of rules. It is there that we come to know the love of God in Jesus Christ as saving sacrifice, warm acceptance, total affirmation, and resounding reconciliation.

It is at the table of the Lord and in the bread which sits thereupon that we come to know the true meaning of God's grace. I've never seen this more clearly demonstrated than I did when I was doing youth ministry, years ago.

I was the youth pastor of a large, suburban church and we had a fairly robust and enthusiastic youth ministry, especially for the senior high. All of the kids went to the same high school and they all knew each other and, for the most part, liked each other, or at least tolerated each other pretty well.

All but Andrew. Andrew was a nineteen year old junior. An only child, he was nearly as big as me, awkward, a little overweight, and he had a learning disability that had slowed his progress through the private school he attended. His communication skills were hindered by both his intellectual deficit and his basic shyness. He had been in the youth group, showed up at regular meetings, for most of the year but had not participated in any special events, trips, or outings.

Much to our surprise, when it came time to register for the summer mission trip to Appalachia, Andrew's was one of the first registrations returned. All through the Spring of the year he participated in the fund raisers and group building games and exercises but always reluctantly and unenthusiastically. Basically, he just stood there until he was allowed to come over and sit with the adults.

The other kids in the group were never mean or even abrupt to him but when their meager attempts to include him were spurned, they gave up. When we met in the parking lot — about 18 kids and 5 adults — to begin the trip, he chose to ride in the van with my wife and me and our three-year-old son and one-year-old daughter and the luggage and tools rather than with the other kids.

The week went off pretty much without incident and Andrew was, again, a reluctant and unenthusiastic participant in nearly every aspect. When we were painting a house he lasted about an hour before he decided that he couldn't stand to have paint on his hands. He tossed his paint brush in the bucket of solvent and went over and sat in the shade. During evening programs he sat with the adult counselors or managed to find a way to sit by himself. He didn't seem unhappy so much as he was just disinterested and bored. Every night we took communion before turning in and he refused to participate.

I had scheduled the trip so that, on the way home, we could stop for one night in Gatlinburg, Tennessee, to just have fun and enjoy ourselves. The first afternoon we crowded everyone into two vans headed to the Dollywood amusement park. My family allowed that we would be spending the day with Andrew because he felt more comfortable with adults than he did with the kids.

In the parking lot as we were preparing to make our way to the gate I gave them my rules, one of which was that they were to never be alone in the park. They were to stick together in at least pairs and, preferably, small groups. We got to the gate, I paid to get everyone in and turned to see Andrew waiting for me. I silently resigned myself to spending the day with him but before I could say anything one of the boys from the group along with two of the girls came up and grabbed Andrew and began dragging him away with them. I heard one of the girls saying something like, "You do NOT want to spend the day with THEM."

Six hours later we adults were standing near the gate waiting to rendezvous with the group when we saw them coming from a distance. They came in mass, all of them together. They had found a souvenir booth that sold beany hats with helicopter blades on the top and every single one of them, including Andrew, was wearing one. They were giggling and laughing and taking pictures of each other and right in the middle of it all was Andrew, wearing his beany and grinning until I thought his face might explode.

But that's not the best part of the story. This is:

That evening, after supper and telling stories about the day and laughing again, we ended our time on the last night we would be together with some scripture, a prayer, and a very simple, rudimentary service of Holy Communion. Andrew had refused to participate in communion all week so I was a little surprised that when I came to him with the bread he didn't back away. He held out his hands making a bowl, stepped from foot to foot, rocking back and forth and nodding his head as I spoke. "Andrew, the body of Christ, broken for you." With those words his faced opened up into that same grin I had seen at the park and he took the bread and placed it in his mouth and closed his eyes as though this little piece of half stale, metaphorical white bread was the best thing he had ever tasted.

And who knows? Maybe it was.

Proper 15
John 6:51-58

"Living Bread"

"I am the living bread that came down from heaven. Whoever eats of this bread will live forever; and the bread that I will give for the life of the world is my flesh." The Jews then disputed among themselves, saying, "How can this man give us his flesh to eat?" So Jesus said to them, "Very truly, I tell you, unless you eat the flesh of the Son of Man and drink his blood, you have no life in you. Those who eat my flesh and drink my blood have eternal life, and I will raise them up on the last day; for my flesh is true food and my blood is true drink. Those who eat my flesh and drink my blood abide in me, and I in them. Just as the living Father sent me, and I live because of the Father, so whoever eats me will live because of me. This is the bread that came down from heaven, not like that which your ancestors ate, and they died. But the one who eats this bread will live forever."
— John 6:51-58

In my thirty years of ordained ministry and 50 years of church membership, I have discovered that there are five kinds of Christian: Free Riders, Fans, Friends, Followers and Fanatics.

FREE RIDERS are Christians in name only.

If you ask them, they will tell you that they believe in God and Jesus. They know how to answer the questions correctly. God is the creator of the universe. Jesus is the son of God, blah, blah, blah. They aren't sure what any of that means. They don't really think about it.

Most of them belong to churches. That is, they have their name on the membership roll of the church and they do the minimum required to keep it there. They send a check every two years or they show up at worship on Christmas Eve or Easter Sunday. They believe in prayer in schools but not in church.

Sometimes they borrow the tables or chairs for their family reunions or high school graduation parties. And they complain about how the church is always talking about money, about how the church is too political, and how it's too conservative or too liberal.

Their relationship to the church is not unlike their relationship to Kroger or McDonalds. They are consumers of the church's product. They like for it to be there when they need it for a wedding or a funeral or a baptism. They expect the minister to call on them when they are in the hospital. They want the perks of church membership but not the responsibilities.

They like to brag about how even though they belong to the church, they don't really need the church to feel close to God. They can do that out in nature, walking through the woods or sitting on their back porch, drinking coffee and listening to the birds sing.

They like to refer to themselves as being "spiritual but not religious."

They are "free riders."

FANS are enthusiastic admirers of Jesus.

They look upon the Son of God the way people in New York look upon Alex Rodriguez, the way teenage girls look upon Taylor Swift or Miley Cyrus or Lady Gaga.

They admire his talent and abilities — he could sure tell a story and he seemed to have a real knack for miracles. They appreciate his accomplishments — he was the founder of the biggest, most influential religion in the history of the world, after all. (Imagine what he could have done if he would have applied himself to business.) And they are blown away by the level of his commitment — I mean, whoa! Crucifixion? Please!

But they know they aren't that talented and they don't have his abilities, they can't heal the sick or turn water into wine, and public speaking scares them to death.

They know they'll never be able to achieve what he achieved. How many people get to start world religions? A dozen maybe? In the history of the world.

And as far as commitment goes, well, how often do we get a chance to die for our faith? And, even if we did have the opportunity, does anyone really expect that of anyone anymore? I mean, isn't that what those crazy people over in the Middle East are doing? And who wants to be like them?

No, it's sufficient to be a fan. It's safe and, though it requires some effort, it's not anything like fanatical. You just learn the jargon, wear the symbols from time to time, sing the fight song and the alma mater when everyone else does and you're in.

Those are the "fans" of Jesus.

The FRIENDS of Jesus that I speak of here are not friends in the traditional sense, more like "Facebook friends."

When you "friend" someone on Facebook, you agree to listen to what they have to say and they agree to listen to what you have to say. No, that's not exactly right.

You agree to be available to listen to what they say even if you don't actually, really listen to it. Or, in the case of Facebook, read it. It works like this:

You and I both have Facebook accounts. But we never cross paths, we never hear from each other unless we "friend" each other. That is, we press a little button that says we will make ourselves available to each other — not in any real way, just on Facebook.

So, now that we're Facebook friends, everything I type on my site goes to you and everything you type on your site goes to me and, presumably, we stay in touch with each other that way. We hear about each other's lives, see pictures of each other's families, hear each other's opinions, laugh at each other's jokes, we say comforting things to each other when one or the other of us is sad or depressed and we say encouraging things to each other when one or the other of us is happy.

About 90% of the communications that take place on Facebook are brief, silly, shallow, and, pretty much, meaningless. It's just for fun.

Through Facebook I'm able to keep track of my nephews, nieces, cousins, their kids, and old friends from high school, college, seminary, and former churches.

These aren't real friendships. We don't bear each other's burdens. We just stay in touch.

And there are Christians who want that kind of Christianity. They don't want a real relationship with God or Jesus Christ or a Christian community and all that that entails, the responsibilities, the commitments, the work, the effort. They want to be Facebook friends. They want to stay in touch with Jesus and they are willing to sit in the pew or read the Bible and be an audience for him, as long as, from time to time, he's willing to return the favor.

FOLLOWERS of Jesus take the relationship to the next level.

They are not content to be just fans, wearing the garb, talking the lingo, singing the songs and then forgetting about it when they hit the parking lot and the drive home.

They are not even content to be Facebook Friends with Jesus, just listening to him and expecting him to listen to them in return.

They listen to Jesus and then they actually try to do what he says to do. They are willing to, from time to time, actually try out the life that Jesus commends to them – the love, the charity, the faith, the trust, the hope. They actually try, whenever they can, to be like Jesus.

Whenever it's appropriate and not too risky, they do what Jesus says to do.

Whenever it's not too expensive and they can be reasonably sure of success they act the way Jesus said to act.

Whenever it doesn't take them too far away from their goals or their chosen destination, they are willing to actually follow the "road less traveled."

They are not unlike Solomon.

Today's Old Testament reading is the story of Solomon's ascendancy to the throne of his father, David.

The reading begins at I Kings 12:10-12, then it skips thirty five verses and goes to Chapter 3 verses 3-14 wherein Solomon asks God to bless his reign as king and God offers Solomon whatever he asks for. Solomon, of course, asks for wisdom, which is the magic word because when he says it all the sirens go off and the fireworks explode and God congratulates him for choosing well and gives him wisdom and everything else that he could have asked for but didn't – power, wealth, fame, women, the whole ball of wax.

Only, what, I wondered, did the lectionary committee leave out when they skipped over those thirty five verses back in chapter two. So I went back there and read those verses and here's what I discovered:

Solomon executes Adonijah, his brother;

Solomon executes Joab, David's cousin;

Solomon executes Shimei, who cursed David;

Solomon executes anyone who questions his right or ability to hold the throne;

Solomon fires and replaces Abiathar, the high priest; and Solomon signs a treaty with Egypt and marries the daughter of Pharaoh to seal a peace treaty between their countries and takes her back with him to live in Jerusalem just to make sure Pharaoh doesn't go back on his word.

Then and only then, when he is firmly seated on the throne, when his detractors and challengers have all been fired or executed and when the only country big and powerful enough to be a threat has signed a treaty and he is holding the daughter of Pharaoh in his palace as a guarantee that the treaty will be kept...then, he is ready to ask God for wisdom and follow God's advice.

Well, at least he did ask for wisdom. At least at some point he decided that slash and burn and kill and threaten and intimidate was no way to rule a country and maybe he ought to ask what God had to say on the subject. So give him credit for that. He may have come late to the wisdom party but at least he came, he showed up.

And so it is with those who are FOLLOWERS of Jesus as we have described them, here. They may not be perfect in their devotion, they may want to put off the difficult parts of following Jesus until their financial picture is secure, or the kids have moved out, or until the economy recovers or the dog dies, but at least they want to follow Jesus. They actually do make the effort to behave as Jesus said to behave, and good for them.

It's just that there is another level, a level of devotion more perfect even than that of the follower. And while it sounds a little off putting, it is, I think, the most perfect level of all.

Let's call this follower of Jesus the FANATIC.

I know that fanaticism is usually thought of as a negative, something to be rejected, eschewed and avoided, but allow me a moment to explain what I mean in this context.

First, let me acknowledge that in the English language the word "fan" was, at one time, just the short form of the word "fanatic." The two words meant, virtually, the same thing. Of course, that is no longer the case. Fans are rarely fanatics and fanatics are something quite different from your run-of-the-mill fans.

As a friend of mine explained it, a fan is someone who dresses up like Brutus Buckeye on certain Saturdays in the fall of the year. A fanatic is someone who has a tattoo of Brutus Buckeye the size of a dinner plate on his chest.

Now, what I am going to suggest is that, in today's gospel lesson from the sixth chapter of John, Jesus is, in fact, calling us beyond being a fan, beyond being a friend, even beyond being a follower. Jesus is calling us to be fanatics in our devotion to him and the message that he brings. He uses a metaphor to make this important point and the metaphor is that of bread.

Like Bread

Bread, in the Middle East is, today, a mainstay of life, even as it was 2,000 years ago. Hardly the fluffy, white stuff we use to make our bologna sandwiches, this is tough, grainy, nutritious stuff, filled with vitamins, necessary carbohydrates and fiber.

In the time of Jesus, as today, the local bread was what we would call large pita bread, flat disks about 10-18 inches in diameter, and an adult man could be expected to eat as many as three in a meal. Prisoners, however, were given one a day. The bread was also used as a spoon to scoop meats and stews from clay pots. Flat and unleavened, it was dry, durable and filling and usually had to be soaked in flavored olive oil to make it palatable. By the first century the Romans had introduced variety and artistry to the Middle Eastern science of bread making. Barley, rye, wheat, corn and other grains were being used and leavening, salt, and sugar were making bread lighter, tastier, and more digestible though it was still far from what we know as bread, today. Roman bread was heavy, dense and grainy.

And in both cases, whether we are talking about European bread or Middle Eastern bread, it was the staff of life and the mainstay of most people's daily diets, especially those who could not afford meat on a regular basis, who had to sell the fish they caught in order to pay for other necessities, and for whom fruits and vegetables were rare, seasonal treats.

Bread is mentioned over 390 times in the Bible, 85 times in the New Testament, twenty of those in the gospel of John (the most of any New Testament book). Of the twenty times John uses the word "bread," seventeen of them occur in the sixth chapter. Four of those are preceded by the words, "I am."

In the RSV and KJV the Hebrew words for bread and food are often used interchangeably which indicates how much bread was a mainstay of the daily diet. Bread is often referred to as the "staff" of life because it was something that people leaned on for nutritional support as a shepherd might lean on his staff.

To be out of or "without bread" was the lowest form of poverty and often a metaphor for hopelessness.

In the Old Testament bread is used as a metaphor for anything that might have an effect on a person's life, good or bad, but in the New Testament bread is used metaphorically only to refer to the coming kingdom of God or to Jesus himself.

By the time of the early church corporate worship usually took place around the meal table where bread was broken and the phrase "breaking bread" came to mean both eating together and worshipping together.

With bread that important to the daily existence of his audience, it is not surprising that Jesus would choose it as an abiding metaphor for his life, his ministry, and the relationship he had with his followers. And John devotes an entire chapter (6), 71 verses of his gospel to that metaphor.

Think for a moment about what happens when you eat a piece of bread.

It is digested and becomes part of you. You and the bread become one, inseparable. It supplies you with nutrients that are necessary for living and you, by eating the bread, enable it to fulfill its purpose, to provide nutrition.

Jesus says that our relationship with him is to be not unlike the relationship we have with the bread that we eat at our meals. We are to take him into our lives and he is to become part of who we are. We are to become as inseparable from Jesus Christ as we are from the bread we ate for breakfast, today.

It is no longer enough to admire Jesus.

It is no longer sufficient to listen and talk to him like a Facebook Friend.

It is no longer satisfactory to try to follow him whenever we have the time and the energy to do so.

We are called, in this passage, beyond all of that to a new level of total commitment.

Christianity is not just a good idea. It's not just one ethical road among many. Jesus is not just our Facebook Friend or our moral trailblazer.

Christianity is a radically different way of living and relating to the world around us. It is challenging and demanding and expensive and hard. It is scandalous in its implications and downright scary in its requirements. It calls us to question everything we thought we knew and every assumption we ever made or accepted.

Jesus puts this all in plain language when he says that "unless you eat the flesh of the Son of Man and drink his blood you have no life in you." Nothing was more abhorrent to first century Jews than breaking the dietary restrictions set down in Leviticus and chief among those was that no human was ever to drink blood of any kind or eat human flesh under any circumstances. Even to use human flesh and blood as a metaphor, as Jesus does here, was a horrible breech of propriety. And, yet, it is this very metaphor that Jesus chooses to show the radical demand of Christianity — demands that would be taken up only by a fanatic.

But, uncomfortable as it may make us, fanatical is exactly what Jesus is calling us to be.

FANTATICAL in our devotion to him; FANATICAL in our commitment to his way; FANATICAL in our acceptance of God's grace and Good News; FANATICAL in our affection for each other; FANATICAL in our care for the broke and the broken; FANATICAL in our allegiance to his kingdom; FANATICAL in our dedication to peace; FANATICAL in our faith; FANATICAL in our hope; FANATICAL in our love.

This, says Jesus in the Gospel of John, is life lived abundantly, authentically, eternally. This is what is given to us if we will but eat of the true Bread of Life.

Appendix

Judaism 101
Shabbat (Sabbath)
(http://www.jewfaq.org/shabbat.htm)

The Nature of Shabbat

Shabbat is the most important ritual observance in Judaism. It is the only ritual observance instituted in the Ten Commandments. It is also the most important special day, even more important than Yom Kippur. This is clear from the fact that more aliyot (opportunities for congregants to be called up to the Torah) are given on Shabbat than on any other day.

Shabbat is primarily a day of rest and spiritual enrichment. The word "Shabbat" comes from the root Shin-Beit-Tav, meaning to cease, to end, or to rest.

Shabbat is not specifically a day of prayer. Although we do pray on Shabbat, and spend a substantial amount of time in synagogue praying, prayer is not what distinguishes Shabbat from the rest of the week. Observant Jews pray every day, three times a day. See Jewish Liturgy. To say that Shabbat is a day of prayer is no more accurate than to say that Shabbat is a day of feasting: we eat every day, but on Shabbat, we eat more elaborately and in a more leisurely fashion. The same can be said of prayer on Shabbat.

In modern America, we take the five-day work-week so much for granted that we forget what a radical concept a day of rest was in ancient times. The weekly day of rest has no parallel in any other ancient civilization. In ancient times, leisure was for the wealthy and the ruling classes only, never for the serving or laboring classes. In addition, the very idea of rest each week was unimaginable. The Greeks thought Jews were lazy because we insisted on having a "holiday" every seventh day.

Shabbat involves two interrelated commandments: to remember (zakhor) Shabbat, and to observe (shamor) Shabbat.

Zakhor: To Remember

Remember the Sabbath day to sanctify it (Hebrew: Zakhor et yom ha-Shabbat l'kad'sho) (Exodus 20:8)

We are commanded to remember Shabbat; but remembering means much more than merely not forgetting to observe Shabbat. It also means to remember the significance of Shabbat, both as a commemoration of creation and as a commemoration of our freedom from slavery in Egypt.

In Exodus 20:11, after Fourth Commandment is first instituted, G-d explains, "because for six days, the L-rd made the heavens and the earth, the sea and all that is in them, and on the seventh day, he rested; therefore, the L-rd blessed the Sabbath day and sanctified it." By resting on the seventh day and sanctifying it, we remember and acknowledge that G-d is the creator of heaven and earth and all living things. We also emulate the divine example, by refraining from work on the seventh day, as G-d did. If G-d's work can be set aside for a day of rest, how can we believe that our own work is too important to set aside temporarily?

In Deuteronomy 5:15, while Moses reiterates the Ten Commandments, he notes the second thing that we must remember on Shabbat: "remember that you were a slave in the land of Egypt, and the L-rd, your G-d brought you forth from there with a mighty hand and with an outstretched arm; therefore the L-rd your G-d commanded you to observe the Sabbath day."

What does the Exodus have to do with resting on the seventh day? It's all about freedom. As I said before, in ancient times, leisure was confined to certain classes; slaves did not get days off. Thus, by resting on Shabbat, we are reminded that we are free. But in a more general sense, Shabbat frees us from our weekday concerns, from our deadlines and schedules and commitments. During the week, we are slaves to our jobs, to our creditors, to our need to provide for ourselves; on Shabbat, we are freed from these concerns, much as our ancestors were freed from slavery in Egypt.

We remember these two meanings of Shabbat when we recite kiddush (the prayer over wine sanctifying Shabbat or a holiday). Friday night kiddush refers to Shabbat as both zikaron l'ma'aseih v'rei'shit (a memorial of the work in the beginning) and zeikher litzi'at Mitz'rayim (a remembrance of the exodus from Egypt).

Shamor: To Observe

Observe the Sabbath day to sanctify it (Hebrew: Shamor et yom ha-Shabbat l'kad'sho) (Deuteronomy 5:12)

Of course, no discussion of Shabbat would be complete without a discussion of the work that is forbidden on Shabbat. This is another aspect of Shabbat that is grossly misunderstood by people who do not observe it.

Most Americans see the word "work" and think of it in the English sense of the word: physical labor and effort, or employment. Under this definition, turning on a light would be permitted, because it does not require effort, but a rabbi would not be permitted to lead Shabbat services, because leading services is his employment. Jewish law prohibits the former and permits the latter. Many Americans therefore conclude that Jewish law doesn't make any sense.

The problem lies not in Jewish law, but in the definition that Americans are using. The Torah does not prohibit "work" in the 20th century English sense of the word. The Torah prohibits "melachah" (Mem-Lamed-Alef-Kaf-Hei), which is usually translated as "work," but does not mean precisely the same thing as the English word. Before you can begin to understand the Shabbat restrictions, you must understand the word "melachah."

Melachah generally refers to the kind of work that is creative, or that exercises control or dominion over your environment. The word may be related to *"melekh"* (king; Mem-Lamed-Kaf). The quintessential example of melachah is the work of creating the universe, which G-d ceased from on the seventh day. Note that G-d's work did not require a great physical effort: he spoke, and it was done.

The word *melachah* is rarely used in scripture outside of the context of Shabbat and holiday restrictions. The only other repeated use of the word is in the discussion of the building of the sanctuary and its vessels in the wilderness. (Exodus 31, 35-38.) Notably, the Shabbat restrictions are reiterated during this discussion (Exodus 31:13), thus we can infer that the work of creating the sanctuary had to be stopped for Shabbat. From this, the rabbis concluded that the work prohibited on *Shabbat* is the same as the work of creating the sanctuary. They found 39 categories of forbidden acts, all of which are types of work that were needed to build the sanctuary:

1. Sowing 2. Plowing 3. Reaping 4. Binding sheaves 5. Threshing 6. Winnowing 7. Selecting 8. Grinding 9. Sifting 10. Kneading 11. Baking 12. Shearing wool 13. Washing wool 14. Beating wool 15. Dyeing wool 16. Spinning 17. Weaving 18. Making two loops 19. Weaving two threads 20. Separating two threads 21. Tying 22. Untying 23. Sewing two stitches 24. Tearing 25. Trapping 26. Slaughtering 27. Flaying 28. Salting meat 29. Curing hide 30. Scraping hide 31. Cutting hide up 32. Writing two letters 33. Erasing two letters 34. Building 35. Tearing a building down 36. Extinguishing a fire 37. Kindling a fire 38. Hitting with a hammer 39. Taking an object from the private domain to the public, or transporting an object in the public domain. (Mishnah Shabbat, 7:2)

All of these tasks are prohibited, as well as any task that operates by the same principle or has the same purpose. In addition, the rabbis have prohibited handling any implement that is intended to perform one of the above purposes (for example, a hammer, a pencil or a match) unless the tool is needed for a permitted purpose (using a hammer to crack nuts when nothing else is available) or needs to be moved to do something permitted (moving a pencil that is sitting on a prayer book), or in certain other limited circumstances. Objects that may not be handled on Shabbat are referred to as "muktzeh," which means, "that which is set aside," because you set it aside (and don't use it unnecessarily) on Shabbat.

The rabbis have also prohibited travel, buying and selling, and other weekday tasks that would interfere with the spirit of Shabbat. The use of electricity is prohibited because it serves the same function as fire or some of the other prohibitions, or because it is technically considered to be "fire."

The issue of the use of an automobile on Shabbat, so often argued by non-observant Jews, is not really an issue at all for observant Jews. The automobile is powered by an internal combustion engine, which operates by burning gasoline and oil, a clear violation of the Torah prohibition against kindling a fire. In addition, the movement of the car would constitute transporting an object in the public domain, another violation of a Torah prohibition, and in all likelihood the car would be used to travel a distance greater than that permitted by rabbinical prohibitions. For all these reasons, and many more, the use of an automobile on Shabbat is clearly not permitted.

As with almost all of the commandments, all of these Shabbat restrictions can be violated if necessary to save a life.

www.ingramcontent.com/pod-product-compliance
Lightning Source LLC
Chambersburg PA
CBHW071726090426
42738CB00009B/1897